In Search of Andreas Vesalius
The Quest for the Lost Grave

In Search of Andreas Vesalius
The Quest for the Lost Grave

Theo Dirix

Translated from Dutch into English by Friends of Vesalius

With three occasional poems:

1902, Edith Wharton: 'Vesalius in Zante (1564)'
1964, Crysanthi Zitsaia: 'To the great Belgian anatomist Andreas Vesalius'
2014, Bryan W. Green: 'Vesalius'

LANNOO CAMPUS

For Omer Steeno, Maurits Biesbrouck and Theodoor Goddeeris,
the éminences grises of Vesalius research in Belgium.

D/2014/45/486 - ISBN 978 94 014 2138 6 - NUR 680, 870

Vormgeving cover: De Witlofcompagnie
Vormgeving binnenwerk: theSWitch

Uitgeverij LannooCampus maakt deel uit van Lannoo Uitgeverij,
de boeken- en multimediadivisie van Uitgeverij Lannoo nv.

Uitgeverij LannooCampus
Erasme Ruelensvest 179 bus 101
3001 Leuven
België
www.lannoocampus.be

Table of Contents

In contrast to the black-and-white original
of the *Fabrica*'s actual title page,
this oversized reproduction of the scene of public dissection
came to life on canvas with the vivid colours used by the artist.
Although the painting at first appeared complete,
Eli realised that its central figure was missing.
Vesalius had yet to be painted,
the entire piece suspended in time
with a captive audience awaiting the anatomist's arrival.

from *Public Anatomy* by A. Scott Pearson,
Ocean View Publishing, Longboat Key, Florida, 2011, pp.164

Illus. 1: Title page of the Fabrica of Vesalius.

1. Digging in the past for a future

On a quiet summer's day in 2013 an email dropped into my inbox at the embassy: 'There are excavations underway on the corner of Kolokotroni Street and Kolyva Street. I've no idea why they are digging there. All I know is that a piece of the old square has been found. The square was situated between the church and the monastery. Did you know about this?'

My search for the lost tomb of the 16th-century anatomist of Brabant, Andreas Vesalius, had often taken me to this part of Zakynthos. In fact, barely two months before receiving this email I had organised a reconnaissance mission to this very corner of the popular Ionian island.

This mission had been agreed in April with the urban and archaeological services and included the participation of Jan Driessen, professor at the Université Catholique de Louvain and Director of the EBSA (École Belge d'Athènes/Belgische School te Athene) and Dr. Apostolos Sarris, Deputy Director of the Institute for Mediterranean Studies – Foundation for Research and Technology, Hellas (IMS- FORTH).

The high expectations of these guests were unfortunately not fulfilled by this visit. I'm afraid I had been a little too enthusiastic in my praise of the island, for the three hours that they were my captive audience during the car ride from Athens to the ferry port of Kyllini.

The Santa Maria delle Grazie Church, for example, where Greek blogger and outstanding historian Pavlos Plessas believes the tomb of Vesalius to have been, was completely gone and nothing but asphalt and houses fill the place where it used to be.

An earthquake in August 1953 had destroyed the entire island and the Saint Nicholas Church, on the central Solomos Square was the only church, from the age of Vesalius, to survive. The Saint Dionysios Church, which was built in a later period, also remained. The rest of the city (including the church of Santa Maria) had been, once again, destroyed. I write 'once again', for in previous times, December 1820 and January 1893, to be precise, the tectonic plates under the island had scraped against each other with the same destructive force and disastrous results. Eternity only lasts sixty years on Zakynthos, wrote the Dutch poet Mark Boog in 2012.

After intensive investigations in the neighbourhood, with old and new maps in hand, Pavlos Plessas is now convinced that the former Catholic church is indeed to be found at this very location. On approaching from the sea, Kolokotroni Street is seen to widen, unexpectedly, just before the crossroad with Kolyva Street, which runs parallel to the coast, and to narrow again immediately after the intersection. It is at this junction on the left-hand side that the works have been going on. A few years ago, during the construction of the second house on the right-hand side, some marble slabs were found and preserved.

They would definitely appear to be part of funerary monuments from inside, or beside, the church. Plessas has himself seen and photographed these marble slabs. Alongside this high building there are two wooden cottages, which date back to just after the great earthquake of 1953.

Next to the works is a free parking place. It is owned by the Chamber of Industry and Commerce, and is, provisionally, rented as a car park by the four-star Hotel Palatino, which is just across the street. There is a garden behind the car park, just around the corner.

In this area, the archaeologists saw little possibility to explore under ground. The chances to excavate at this location are small, except perhaps in the gardens or if ever the wooden houses were to be demolished. Opportunities would have also arisen of course, in the parking lot, if and when the Chamber of Commerce and Industry would build their offices.

None of us could have imagined, therefore, that only a few weeks later, at the same location and totally unexpectedly, a fairly recent house was knocked down. Furthermore, it was unthinkable that the excavation works that were carried out after this were in fact the four-feet-deep foundations for a new building.

Having twice reread Pavlos Plessas's email, which he had sent from his second home in London, I decided to call the vice-mayor of Zakynthos, Akis Ladikos.

He is the Vice-Mayor of Culture, Sports and Youth Affairs and is also passionate about archeology. I could not get through to him, as he was at a meeting, but moments later I had his employee, Dimitris, on the line and he translated into English the following answers from Ladikos:

'The archaeological department has, indeed, been doing some digging, but has not found anything more than a few rocks, discovered four metres deep. These were probably part of the defence wall, and not from the church itself.'

By making light of their activities and discoveries, he unintentionally fueled my frustration.

I didn't feel at all comfortable about this call. I overcame my reluctance and determined to phone David Lomastro, who is a colleague of mine at the embassy. As luck would have it, he had chosen to spend his month's holiday on Zakynthos, with his family and friends, who had flown by charter plane directly from Belgium, and was, at the very moment of my call, about to take a walk into the town. On hearing my story, he was happy to make a slight detour and to take a few photographs of the site. Half an hour later I was able to load snapshots of bulldozers and concrete mixers onto the screen in my office.

My colleague, known for his ironic sense of humour, commented, 'I thought archaeologists always worked with a brush and tweezers!"

It wasn't apparent from the photos that the archaeological services had been involved, but it was very obvious that major earthworks were underway here, and that a crater had been filled with concrete in preparation for a new construction.

Along with a brief request for more information, I sent the photos to the Director of the Department of Byzantine Archaeology in Patras, Anita Koumousi. Her office is in the port city in the Peloponnese, just across from the island. As the leading post on Zakynthos is not filled at present, she has, quite recently, been made responsible for the island. In preparation for our April mission I had tried for months, unsuccessfully I'm afraid, to make an appointment with her. She had informed me, by mail, that she had never been to Zakynthos and that she hadn't heard of Vesalius before I mentioned him. She had, however, pledged me all the support available from her colleagues in the Byzantine Museum at Solomos Square.

Meanwhile, my correspondent Pavlos Plessas, and his informant on the island, told me that the answer to their questions about the nature of the works had been given very clearly: there were no archaeological excavations taking place at this location.

The reaction of the archaeological department came a few days later. Mrs Koumousi had especially travelled to Zakynthos and had personally supervised the excavation work. This is what she wrote to me: 'At first glance, I am sure that what was found, at a depth of two metres, is part of a weak wall, built at a late stage, probably 19th century. If a relic of Santa Maria delle Grazie is to be found it will certainly be a lot deeper and of a different building structure, but we keep on hoping.'

The following days were very busy with mails passing back and forth, but Pavlos Plessas remained doubtful about the information we received.

'If she says two metres deep, which Santa Maria is she referring to? The 16th century one, or the 1953 one? The 1953 one was higher than the street level of today. Was the floor of the church removed and raised each time the church was rebuilt? And what is two metres deep? The bottom of the wall or the top? Or was there only one layer remaining? I am sure this is not the wall of the church – it is located too much to the south. Perhaps it is part of the outer wall, but only if the brickwork is close to Kolokotroni Street. Walls from the 16th century served as reinforcements and therefore were thick, but that of course depended upon the materials available. No news of the director or deputy mayor? The excavation works must have been completed then?'

The excavation works were indeed soon ended, the foundations poured and the hole filled in.

Six months later I was back at this site, this time to view the concrete skeleton of a four-storey building! From the corner of the intersection, the new structure even encroached on part of the car park of the hotel. As with any new construction, a building permission, several authorizations and a control visit of the site from the Archaeological Department must have been applied for, months and months ahead. How strange that nobody has mentioned this during our visit.

In some areas in Greece you have only to stick a shovel into the ground to stumble upon history. For construction in areas where archaeological remains are considered probable, a permit must be received before work can commence. If old stones are stumbled upon, the owner must inform the archaeological department immediately in order for an emergency investigation to take place. The owner is obliged, by law, to co-operate fully in the protection of both the site and anything found on it. Depending on the importance of the find, building works may be temporarily or permanently shut down.

This law has given rise to an ambiguous attitude towards archaeology. Greeks are so spoiled, from the historical point of view, that old stones are often considered to be a nuisance.

The media interest in our search for the grave of Vesalius meant that the procedure regarding this construction was followed very carefully indeed. Instead of calling out a technician from the local archeological department, the director came personally from Patras. During our exploratory mission, everybody had heard us talk about the fact that the church was located on the other side of the crossroad, thus the excavation works were completed with confidence.

The search for the lost tomb of Andreas Vesalius, who was buried half a millennium ago, would not be completed on that summer's day in 2013. The area, that only sixty years earlier had suffered another devastating earthquake, the aftermath of which resulted in the stone waste of an entire neighbourhood – houses, church, cemetery and monastery – being bulldozed into the sea, did not give up its secrets yet.

Very recently, however, by way of titillation, a simply decorated, stone artefact from the church emerged, and was found by accident in front of the site on Kolokontroni Street, on the side nearest to the sea. Just to keep the fires going!

For the Embassy of Belgium in Athens, this story had in fact begun in March 2011. (An earlier approach from Pascale Pollier, the medical artist who started this quest for the grave of Vesalius, had been given a rather lukewarm reception by my predecessors at the Embassy.) My involvement started quite soon after my arrival in Greece, on being introduced to Steven Soetens in March, who was then the director of the Ecole Belge/Belgische School at Athens, the EBSA.

'You might want to contact Pascale Pollier,' he wrote to me after our first meeting. 'It occurred to me on my way back to the school that we could perhaps combine a couple of things. There is the occasion of 500 years Vesal (as they call Vesalius here). Maybe a new monument could be made, perhaps in collaboration with the artist. With the presence of the Embassy on Zakynthos, perhaps we could help with the organization of an event, with an exhibition (I hear that plans are already being made). This is Pascale's email address. It's just an idea!' He wrote prophetically.

Pascale Pollier immediately responded to my message of April 1 with a serious and enthusiastic message: 'We would be delighted to collaborate with the Belgian School and the Embassy of Belgium. We are planning a major conference in 2014 (probably in Brussels) with the provisional title 'Vesalius Continuum'.

This would be in collaboration with: the Association Européenne des Illustrateurs Medicaux et Scientifique (Association of Medical and Scientific Illustrators of Europe) (AEIMS), the Medical Artists's Association of Great Britain (MAA) and The Vesalius Trust. We will keep you informed of our plans.'

I was infected, infected with the Vesalius Bug. Vesalius became a very regular feature in the newsletters that the Embassy sends to the Belgian community in Greece. For inspiration I corresponded with ever-increasing intensity with Pascale Pollier and Ann Van de Velde, both of the association of Biological and Medical Art in Belgium (BIOMAB). Electronic news letters are known to be peculiar and unpredictable and like a message in a bottle, they came the way of Professor Em. Dr. Omer Steeno. He is a specialist physician in internal medicine, an endocrinologist and an andrologist, Associate Professor and the emeritus Head of Clinic in Leuven. He has devoted his life to the study of Vesalius. With more than fifty publications on the anatomist, he is one of the most eminent Vesalius scholars in Belgium.

'Ready for further collaboration,' he generously offered his assistance. I've since abused his kind offer to such an extent that I gained not just one, but three new friends. Many articles on Vesalius are a collaboration between Maurice Biesbrouck, MD and clinical biologist from Roeselare, Theodoor Goddeeris, a medical doctor from Kortrijk, and Omer Steeno, from Leuven. Without this infernal trio, this book would not exist. When I playfully questioned if this nickname bothered them at all, my namesake responded, 'We are like the three-headed Cerberus, watching over everything said about Vesalius.'

Pascale Pollier and her fellow enthusiasts were delighted with the suggestion that the conference be held on Zakynthos rather than in Brussels.

On August 30th, 2011, with a copy sent to Omer Steeno, came a request from the UK. Mark Richard Gardiner, retired British professor of paediatrics, on behalf of The Hellenic Medical Society of the United Kingdom, expressed his desire to be involved in the Vesalius project. In October 2011, I sent the request on to Pascale Pollier, who had settled back into London, and had sadly lost her address book and correspondents lists. Gardiner, fortunately, has since opened his address book for the Vesalius Continuum Conference on Zakynthos and has shared with us his list of contacts. On this list are some of the most prestigious names in the academic world.

Thus a great team of collaborators has slowly accumulated and together we have worked on plans for an international conference on science and art, an exhibition, a new memorial monument to Vesalius, and a series of concerts in the Ionian Islands. The quest for the lost grave of the anatomist is what brought us together. By offering patronage for the festivities, the Belgian Embassy in Athens, with the blessing of the City of Zakynthos, is continuing a tradition created by previous diplomats, who saw in Vesalius a bridge between Belgium and Greece, between past and present.

The grand occasion to bring all these activities together: the 500th celebration of Vesalius's birth in Brussels and the 450th anniversary of his death in Zakynthos in 2014/2015.

2. Andreas Vesalius Bruxellensis

On December 31, 1514, Isabel Crabbe gave birth to a son in Brussels, the second of three boys, (she had three sons and a daughter), who was named after his father, Andries van Wesele.

A pharmacist by profession, Andries the elder worked in the service of the Habsburger from Ghent, for him with the protruding chin: Charles, Landlord of the Netherlands, later to become the Roman Emperor, Charles the Fifth. The grandfather of the young Andries, named Everaert, and his great-grandfather, Johannes, or Jan van Wesele, were doctors at the court of Mary of Burgundy, Queen of the Netherlands, who still ruled our region. Great-grandfather Johannes was also dean of the medical faculty of the University of Leuven and later chief physician of the City of Brussels.

I have since learned from Omer Steeno, that in the wedding hall of Brussels, our capital city, there is a wooden statue of great-grandfather Johannes.

The property owned by Johannes, and later his son Everaert, lay on the edge of the Meerdaalwoud, in the area now called Oud-Heverlee, between the lakes of the domain known today as Zoete Waters (Sweet Waters). Now a restaurant, called Spaans Dak (Spanish Roof), a plaque hangs on the wall recording that here was the family domain called Heerlijkheid Steenbergen, the cradle of Andries.

It was a wintery day when Omer Steeno showed me a photo posted on the Internet, in which he and Maurice Biesbrouck pose, with great pride, in front of the plaque.

According to my sources, grandfather Everaert van Wesele died unmarried, with three 'bastard children', who could not, therefore, inherit the property. The property, 'De Heerlijkheid' went instead to his sister and three brothers.

The lunch that Steeno and I enjoyed at the Spaans Dak restaurant was excellent and marked the beginning of our tradition of sharing a table and talking endlessly about Vesalius.

He told me that Oud-Heverlee had slowly built up a close relationship with Zakynthos in the second half of the nineties. After an intense correspondence in April 1998 a first visit took place.

Steeno led a delegation of four to the Greek island. He was accompanied by Constant Boghe (tourism), Rachael Clabots (culture) and Albert Vanhamel (member of the city council). Their translator was Vivi Labordus-Papachristou. They were received by Fotis Ladikos, who was the mayor at the time. On looking at the pictures of the trip, delegation on an outing, delegation at the table, delegation gets present, the striking features of Fotis Ladikos show that he is undeniably the father of Akis Ladikos, the current Deputy Mayor of Culture.

Various practical objections stood in the way of the dream of twinning the towns – or was the interest too one-sided?

The twinning between Zakynthos and Oud-Heverlee may have got off to a bad start; however we succeeded, in early 2014, in creating a school exchange between the 1st Lyceum of Zakynthos and The Sacred Heart Institute in Heverlee. The two-year programme, with visits back and forth, was funded by the European Comenius Fund. It was our intention to enable young people from both countries to step in the footsteps of a European *avant la lettre*. We have always believed that the inspiration of a revolutionary and innovative researcher/teacher from the past can guarantee a great enhancement of the future. The idea to involve students was first suggested to us by Gardiner. He was perhaps thinking along the lines of focusing on medical studies, and Pascale Pollier too would love to involve future medical artists in the project. It can never begin too early, I suggested to the contrary, and after this exchange, students from both secondary schools might perhaps choose to study medicine, or the history of science, or art and science. (Alternatively, as I reflected playfully to their parents during an information session at Heverlee, they might, rather more disturbingly, go for consular or diplomatic sciences.)

The van Weseles were the descendants of a merchant family from the German city of Wesel, on the Rhine. On the red diamond of the city's coat of arms there are three weasels around a silver shield. On the Vesalius coat of arms the weasels are placed below each other. This coat of arms adorns the frontispiece on the title page of his most famous book: *De humani corporis fabrica libri septem, (On the fabric of the human body in seven books)*. Thanks to Chantal Pollier, sculptor and designer of the plinth of a new memorial statue created by her sister Pascale and Richard Neave, it also appears in Zakynthos.

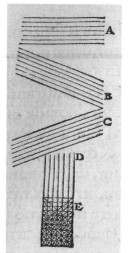

Illus. 2: Pattern of the fibers in a vein wall, details in plate 190 of the Fabrica of Vesalius.

Five hundred years ago, the street in Brussels where Andries van Wesele was born was called Hellestraatken. Today it is named Joseph Dupont Street and is near the European Synagogue in Regentschapslaan. It links the Robert Catteau Lyceum in Ernest Allard Street with Wol Street, which becomes Karmelietenstraat.

This is also my adopted neighbourhood: the Karmelietenstraat is the location of the headquarters of my employer, the Federal Public Service of Foreign Affairs. And on a blue Monday, between two foreign postings, my children went to school in the Robert Catteau Lyceum. In those days I regularly passed by the plaque on the wall of the school in Miniemen Street. The people of the City of Brussels mounted the plaque there on the occasion of the 400th anniversary of the death of their famous fellow townsman, in October 1964. As befits a school that teaches the Classics, the plaque is written in Latin and reads:

'Dignummemoria in hac area Seculo XV surgebat domus perclebris avctoris andreae Vesalii bruxellensis 1515–1564 qui anno 1542 suum humani corporis fabrica celeberumum Librum the feliciter posteris typis mandavit.'

Here was the birthplace of Andreas Vesalius of Brussels 1514–1564 who became world famous in 1542 for his celebrated book about the construction of the human body.

But shouldn't that be 1543? I thought to myself, even then!

Andries van Wesele spent several years of his childhood in Brussels. After primary school, he left Brussels to begin his secondary studies in Leuven.

He, who was born in Brussels and named Andries van Wesele and who died known as Ανδρέα Βεζάλ (Andre Vesal or Bezal) on Zakynthos, would become Andreas Vesalius Bruxellensis in Leuven. There the foundations of his future life were laid, as was 'predicted' by Girolamo Cardano, a successful 16th-century astrologer/physician/mathematician and inventor, who drew a horoscope for his contemporary Andreas Vesalius, as Cardano did for all celebrities of his generation.

Out of a comparison between horoscope and life's journey, he tried to determine the influence of the planets on one's life. He described Andreas as a 'highly admirable expert in the study of the dissection of bodies, as important as the classical scholars'. The astrologer went on to further praise the anatomist's passion and skill, exceptional intellect and fluency, and he prophesied that the son of the Brussels pharmacist would become famous and would be glorified long after his death.

Scientists of the early 16th century did not look down on magic and the occult. Astrology was then as successful a business as it is today, and equally true, am I right? Judging by Cardano's prophetic 'prediction'?

Nonetheless, what is true is that Vesalius was born in a time when two periods of history scraped against and shocked each other like tectonic plates.

3. With the *Fabrica* among dead poets

The anatomist, a magician in his dark robes,
his prostrate lady before him, looks out at us
(what secret will he withdraw next?
the veined balloon of her bladder,
the umber stalk of the umbilicus,
the fetus's tiny froglike foot?)
and raises a finger to bid us *attend*. But it is the skeleton
who presides over this carnival;
he sits on the balcony railing, dead center, staff in hand.
He is regal and captive amid gaiety, at the site
of his own dissection: this room to which bodies
stolen from the gallows are brought and are made
to play their final role, organ by organ, this room which,
with its hyaline dome where at night the stars
of the firmament ring, mimics heaven.

Nadine Sabra Meyer
in the title poem of her debut collection,
The Anatomy Theater,
the title page of De humani corporis fabrica, 2006.

'History can be deadly ironic,' I previously wrote in a printed booklet on Vesalius. 'He, who in his youth was looking for bones in order to study the human body, had his own bones lost on an exotic island.'

In his book, *Island of the Dead*, which is a collection of essays about writers and islands, Dutch author Maarten Asscher describes the island of Zakynthos as that of dead poets. This would certainly apply to, and include, Andreas Vesalius.

In one fell swoop in 1543, Andreas Vesalius became world famous by producing a book about anatomy: *The humani corporis fabrica libri septem (Seven Books on the Construction of the Human Body)*. The books appeared in the same year as Copernicus published his study of the revolving of the heavenly bodies: the *Revolutionibus Orbium Coelstium (On the Revolutions of the Heavenly Spheres)*.

From whatever discipline the book of Vesalius was approached, it was an invaluable reference book, and it is still considered so to this day.

The *Fabrica* was as revolutionary in the scrutiny of the human anatomy as the book of Copernicus was in the knowledge of the universe. Individually they unleashed, at the same time, a turning point in the history of knowledge. Through personal research and observation, they turned irreversibly against uncritical ancient lore.

Vesalius's *magnum opus* is also a pedagogical monument. Written in Latin, it describes body parts with terminology still in use today. Unlike his predecessors, who lectured *ex cathedra* and who would rather not soil their hands with decomposing bodies, Vesalius insisted that he hold the scalpel himself. Whereas illustrations in textbooks are taken for granted today, the concept of an illustrated book was a totally new phenomenon in the time of Vesalius.

The collaboration between Vesalius and Jan Steven van Calcar, a painter and sculptor from the studios of Titian, who illustrated the book with dozens of woodcuts, created a unique work of art.

The images of the body and its parts are, despite their documentary character, captivating and moving. The illustrations are timeless and could even be said to be avant-garde today. The representation of the figures creates a classic picture-language, which becomes a subject in itself. The environments in which they stand or move, both internal and external, also tell their own story.

For example, *The Epitome*, which is Vesalius's 'Fabrica' for students, contains anatomical drawings in which man and woman are portrayed as classical Greek beauties. The man is holding a skull. The couple, who without doubt represent Adam and Eve, could have walked out of a religious or theological text. Is Vesalius suggesting that the man and skull refers to the mortality of man? This was certainly seen to be the case in the copy made by the engraver Thomas Geminus a few years later in his work on anatomy inspired by Vesalius, and in which the man holds an apple and a snake crawls out of a skull lying on the ground.

For Geminus, the religious connotation was very apparent; for Vesalius the cultural prevailed: Eve, the first woman created by God equals the Roman goddess Venus equals the Greek goddess Aphrodite.

Elsewhere Vesalius shows one of his eternal women with abdomen cut open, and there is a striking resemblance to the Aphrodite of Knidos by the classical Athenian sculptor Praxiteles. There is also a male breast in the *Fabrica*, which is derived from the so-called Belvedere torso by the first-century Athenian sculptor 'Apollonius son of Nestor'.

We know that a study of the latter work, from the mid 15th century, was in a Roman collection, and a generation later it came to symbolize the renaissance of classical beauty. Vesalius must have seen this picture, and perhaps even the drawing of the Belverdere torso by his Belgian compatriot Martin Heemskerk.

What is remarkable is that in this work from Vesalius the broken-off arms and legs of the sculpture seem to be responsibly anatomically amputated in the drawings.

I cannot read the densely printed Latin text of the *Fabrica* but, fortunately, Maurice Biesbrouck translated the first book into Dutch, and English translations can be found here and there.

On the occasion of the Vesalius celebrations in 2014, a Dutch translation will be published, in a rare facsimilie edition, by Alfagen, the alumni of the Faculty of Medicine at the KU Leuven.

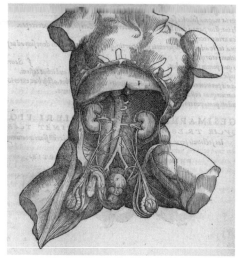

Illustr. 31
Male torso on plate 248 from the Fabrica of Vesalius.

Meanwhile the prestigious Swiss medical and scientific publisher, Karger, has recently released *The Fabric of The Human Body: An annotated translation of the 1543 and 1555 editions* of '*The Humani Corporis Fabrica Libri Septem*', by Daniel H. Garrison and Malcolm H. Hast. Judging from the text, albeit in translation, it appears that we are dealing with a literary work of art.

Images and comparisons of all kinds enrich the text. As for the pictorial imagery, I won't go too deeply into the literary imagery either, suffice to say it is a book full of riches. For one catalog of metaphors, I will, however, open the door a little wider.

Vesalius didn't call his book *The Building of the Human Body* without reason. There are indeed 'affinities of stones and bones", as Pamela O. Long so rightly said in her article on the subject. If I understand anatomy correctly, it is a rather technical and mechanical branch of medicine. It comes as no surprise to me, therefore, that day-to day construction terms are used frequently throughout the book.

In the illustration of the frontispiece of the *Fabrica,* Vesalius stands in centre stage of a crowded dissecting theatre, with his gaze fixed on the reader as he displays a dissected cadaver. Nadine Sabine Mayer, with whose verses I opened this chapter, would no doubt agree on the beauty of this scene, which takes place in a building with full vaulted arches. In this way this refers to his belief that the vertebrae are the keystones in the archway of the back. He continues to make architectural references in the first chapter of Book II, as noticed by Daniel Garrison and Malcolm Hast, in which he describes the muscles and ligaments as the foundations and base for the other body parts.

In two different places in the book, to give another example, a simple hinge of a door adorns the text.

There is, of course, more to this masterpiece than stated thus far. Metaphors, symbolic references and even myths about building and construction works are timeless. As an anatomist, Vesalius showed his affinity for architecture. He also showed this affinity, and maybe even more so, as a Renaissance man, in that the adoration of classical and ancient architecture represented much more than just a love of building techniques.

The frontispiece of the *Fabrica* contains a frieze that is signed by architect Sebastiano Serlio. Indeed, similarities between Vesalius and Serlio are very evident. In *Rhetoric and Medicine in Early Modern Europe*, Stephen Pender and Nancy S. Struever highlight the parallels between the *Humani corporis fabrica* and *I sette libri dell'architettura*:

> 'the division in seven books, the attitude toward classical sources, the place devoted to the communication of knowledge by illustration, the importance accorded to the rapprochement, between theory and practice, the relationship between parts, structures and functions.'

Moreover Serlio was known as a designer of wooden temporary theatres. The print of Vesalius and van Calcar shows plants growing on the column of the vaulted arches, which would seem to indicate that Vesalius did his anatomical research outside. Indeed, Alessandro Benedetti (1445–1525), who was Professor of Anatomy and Surgery in Padua, declared, 'Preliminary anatomical theatres are to be built on spacious grounds and are to be well ventilated, with seats in a circular positioning, around the central stage, similar to the Colosseum of Rome and the Arena of Verona.'

In the plate that shows Vesalius at work, we clearly see that the public is supported by wooden railings in a hemispheric auditorium.

Serlio and Vesalius/van Calcar are radiating the same Zeitgeist. We find in their books almost identical images of classical ruins, arches and bridges. They evoke the classics as inspiration for the study of both architecture and anatomy.

However you look at the *Fabrica*, it is an endless ode to the flesh, a sensual hymn to the body, a canticum to life and death. The book is pure poetry in classical Greco-Roman imagery. Was Vesalius thus destined to end his life abruptly on a Greek island? An island strewn with ruins…

After my visit on May 15ᵗʰ, 2013 a local newspaper said of me: 'As a regular visitor to our island, he is now naturalized. How could it be otherwise? As a student of teacher Akis Ladikos, he leaves no stone unturned, no castle, monument, ruin or crack in a wall.' Inspired by Vesalius/van Calcar, I indeed had made a series of pictures of arches and vaults, of plants growing on walls, and classical building elements scattered in the streets of Zakynthos, stating that this must feel like home for Vesalius.

When, during our reconnaissance mission, I showed archaeologist Apostolos Sarris the many artefacts lying around, he added, 'You could keep school pupils busy here for years and years by assigning them to make an inventory of archaeological remains, and asking them to calculate and to draw these.' I later tried to propose his great idea to the first Lyceum of Zakynthos.

Moreover, on this island of dead poets, Vesalius is in excellent company. There is still plenty of room between the mausoleums in the spacious lobby of the museum named after at least two of them: Dionysios Solomos, Andreas Kalvos and Eminent Zakynthians. In May 2012, I contacted Flemish artist Filip Sterckx, creator of the installation 'Vesalius Revisited', which was shown in 2009 in the Anatomical Theatre of Leuven. On a dissection table was a live model on whom the various stages of dissection were projected. Wouldn't it be nice to bring Vesalius back to life, between the graves of Solomos and Kalvos?

Until the moment Vesalius is given the status of 'eminent naturalized guest' on the island, he is perhaps resting beside the beheaded Roman orator, with severed hands, Cicero. Unfortunately the rest of his remains have also been lost on the island. Imagine for a moment, Vesalius resting next to the idol of his contemporaries.

Or will his restless spirit still wander around the island in the company of local poets, such as Gregory Xenopoulos and Ugo Foskolos? They, like him, were buried in a foreign land, the former in a poor man's grave in Athens, the latter in a graveyard in England, later removed to a crypt in Florence. What is worse, I ask myself, to have no tomb at all, or to be excavated from one and reburied in another?

Perhaps Vesalius is still in the intermediate world, in the company of Lord Byron. Just after he died on Easter Monday in 1824 in Missolonghi in Western Greece, Byron's embalmed body rested on Zakynthos during the month of May. After an endless discussion about his final resting place – be it in Athens or on the island? – his coffin eventually left by boat on a last trip to London. Could it be that this is what Vesalius would want? A final journey home?

What providence let him die in Greece, on an island between the ruins of dead poets? To formulate an answer to this question is like searching for a lost grave in the verses of the poets who have lost theirs a long time ago.

Katerina Demeti, who is the Director of the Museum of Solomos and Kalvos, has told me that the Belgian anatomist lives in the hearts of all the inhabitants of the Greek island and is thus watching over them. Together we reasoned that if this island was the place where he feels most at home, he might not want his bones to be found.

On each official visit to Zakynthos, journalists from the local press ask me the question: 'Do you really think you're going to find him?'

The first time this happened I looked the journalist straight in the eye and gave him this measured answer, 'Of course, I'm sure!'

The second time I heard myself answer that the grave was not as important as the quest. The mouth of the interviewer developed an ironic smile.

The third time I heard, in my head, a cock crow in response and I answered to the tune that as long as we did not find the grave, I had a good reason to continue my visits to my favourite island.

Is it not surprising that this last answer received more than the attention it deserved in a local television show? Furthermore, this sceptical view of my activities is now, I'm sorry to say, shared by the archaeologist of the Byzantine Museum of Zakynthos.

Meanwhile, I can only declare that the tracks which lead to Vesalius's former alleged grave are slowly being wiped out, together with the contours of its landscape, disturbed by new constructions. Newly discovered tracks, on the other hand, which are under old constructions, are rising again.

It was long assumed that Vesalius was washed ashore, onto the deserted beach of Laganas, following a shipwreck. Today that same beach is overrun with thousands of tourists. Only the most curious have an eye for the memorial that was erected here by Greek alumni of Belgian universities. The lettering on the stone was barely legible, eroded by salty sea air. Recently the letters have been given a lick of black paint. When I asked a pharmacist from the Vesal district to point out the road to the memorial, he didn't know what I was talking about. A pharmacist! To know nothing of a fellow man of medicine, an ancestor!

It gets worse. When Omer Steeno visited the beach in 2007, he overheard a guide holding forth and declaring that the monument was established there as a tribute to a doctor who had built the new hospital of Zakynthos, after the Second World War.

Perhaps it would take a solitary tourist to make the connection between the name of the Belgian anatomist and the restaurant on the corner, the hotel on Vesal Street, and the supermarket where he buys his alcohol (which hasn't merely the name Vesal, but 'Super-Vesal-Market').

And so it is that if you ask people how the famous physician and anatomist met his end, most will answer that he was nearly drowned and died having been washed up on a deserted beach.

Many continue to believe that his mortal remains were transferred to the Fransciscan monastery on the hill above the beach of Laganas. That story, however, has little to do with fact and would appear to be mainly made up.

The memorial, placed there in the fifties to designate the possible site of the tomb, was stolen. The police and the courts have recently set up an investigation into the theft, which has as yet not brought anything to light. A building construction on the mythical hill has consequently been stalled, but is very near to the completion of a new villa.

Were the remains of Vesalius perhaps transferred from the monastery to a church in the city? Could that church be the Catholic Santa Marie delle Grazie, the same church where his idol Cicero was previously buried? If so, what would now remain, after everything that church has experienced; it has been looted, turned into an army barracks, blown up, and destroyed several times by earthquakes.

When King Leopold I, just after independence, enquired about the grave of his newly acquired Belgian son, the Greeks had more important things to be concerning themselves with, as they were busy with their own fight for independence. In 1914, Belgian professor Jean-Joseph Tricot-Royer wanted to commemorate the 400th birthday of Vesalius on Zakynthos, but a few weeks after his request the First World War broke out.

During World War II, a seaplane, with the most senior director of the Department of Health of the German Seaforce on board, landed on Zakynthos to search for the grave of Vesalius, who he considered of German descent. We have learned this from the local pharmacist and historian, Nicolas Barbianis, who spent his entire life in the search for the grave of Vesalius, but had all his efforts turned to rubble by the great earthquake of 1953.

In 2011, when we picked up the thread of Barbianis from the sixties, the representatives of the island were denied the official launch of the preparations for 2014, due to a ferryboat strike. During three of my travels, the earth trembled. On the first occasion my wife and I were the only people in the restaurant to look up when our glasses spontaneously started to klink together. On April 23rd, 2013, however, in the middle of the night, with a showing on the Richter scale of a magnitude of 4.2, the epicentre of an earthquake was only 15 kilometres from Zakynthos.

The Ionian Islands and especially the neighbouring island of Kefalonia were again shaken by a countless series of earthquakes and aftershocks in early 2014. The heaviest of these shocks reached a magnitude of almost six on the Richter scale and a state of emergency was declared.

Are these occurrences an indication of what is to come in the year of Vesalius? Sometimes it seems that the search for the lost tomb is reminiscent of the curse of the Pharaohs.

In one of the most famous artworks in Vesalius's acclaimed book, a skeleton is portrayed in a contemplative moment, the many phalanges of his hand resting on the skull of another. What may go through Vesalius's own brain is inscribed on the sarcophagus or altar:

> Vivitur ingenio, Caetera mortis erunt
> Genius lives on, all else is mortal

Whilst I unfold the history of the quest for the grave of the greatest anatomist of all time and hereby hope to make my own personal contribution, a question forms itself and echoes about my ears: does the universal genius wish his skeleton to be found?

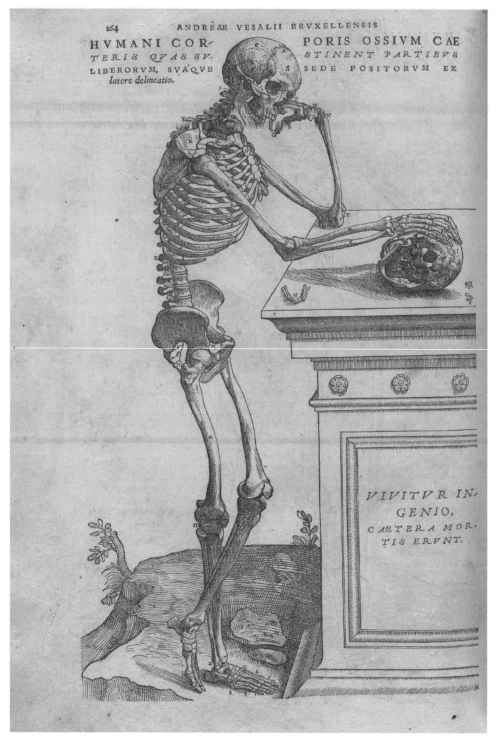

Illus. 4: Skeleton contemplating, plate 93 from the Fabrica of Vesalius.

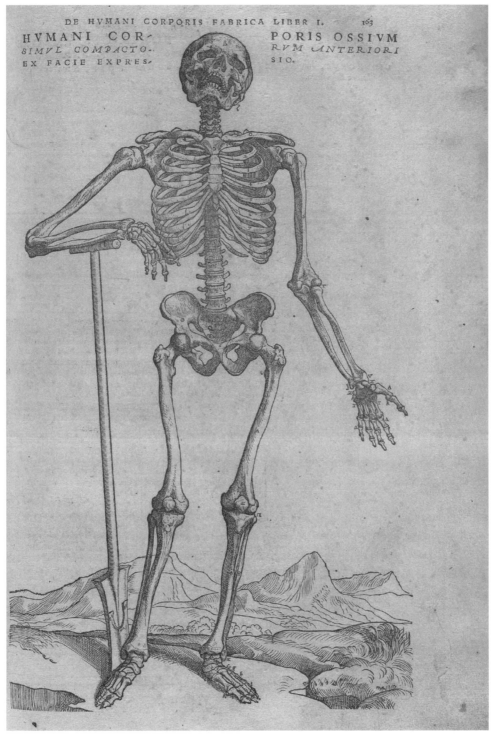

Illus. 5: Skeleton digging, plate 92 from the Fabrica of Vesalius.

4. Portraits versus facial reconstruction

Should we then really,
with bare and bleeding feet,
take a heavy spade in the hand
and stab the stony ground of a foreign land

Charles Baudelaire in 'Skeleton digging'
from *Flowers of Evil, 1857.*

Despite his personal warning that only genius is imperishable and despite the curse that would seem to follow the quest for the grave, what becomes apparent from this story is that no one wants to stop the quest.

It has happened to me a few times now, on Zakynthos, that I get asked the question, 'And haven't you found his grave yet?' Believe it or not, this is music to my ears: indeed I'm just a tombstone tourist, otherwise known – says Wikipedia – as a 'taphophile, a cemetery enthusiast, a grave hunter or a graver'.

This quest, for a lost dead soul, is my life. I'm not sure that the question is meant to bring music; the melody that is sung rather betrays a tone of irony and ridicule. Nevertheless people seem to expect an answer from me. Is it that everyone is attracted by his grave? Now and then I will indeed clumsily try to answer this question, but for now I have to excuse myself, as I must urgently continue my search.

A couple of years ago Italian art historians opened the crypt of Lady Gherardini, because it was believed, by some, that she may have been the model for the Mona Lisa. I assume that artists dream of reconstructing her mysterious smile. Previously permission was given to open the tomb of Leonardo da Vinci, which is in the French Loire Valley. It was hoped that the skull of the Renaissance predecessor of Vesalius would be discovered, enabling researchers to reconstruct the face of da Vinci, and thereby compare it to the face of the Mona Lisa. Was it ever suggested that the Mona Lisa was a self-portrait of da Vinci?

In the summer of that same year, news came from the UK where, under a car park in Leicester, and between medieval stonework from a former Franciscan monastery, a skeleton was discovered. It was later confirmed and then unconfirmed that this was the King of England and the last monarch of the House of York, who died in 1485. Thanks to facial reconstruction, Richard III was, perhaps, a little reborn in 2013.

In March 2014, when a media storm in a tea cup erupted in Belgium, over our search for the grave in the car park on Kolyva Street in Zakynthos, an avid reader tweeted, 'Parking/cemeteries are fashionable… and now even Vesalius!'

As already mentioned, Pascale Pollier, biomedical artist, and Dr. Ann Van de Velde, haematologist and biomedical artist who works under the rather appropriate pseudonym, Sanguine, are the driving forces behind the association of Biological and Medical Art in Belgium, BIOMAB. Along with Antwerp anatomist Dr. Francis Van Glabbeek, they go in search of art in science. They regularly organize exhibitions and drawing sessions of human and animal dissections. The universities of Antwerp and Ghent are open to their proposal to create a real discipline of biomedical art; the illustrators and artists will rely heavily upon the legacy of Andreas Vesalius and the creator of his prints, Jan Steven van Calcar.

In 2009 Pollier completed a course in facial reconstruction in Maastricht. The idea immediately came to her that it would be wonderful to make a reconstruction of the head of Vesalius, but she realized soon that we hardly know what he looked like. She determined that she would set about this with the help of Richard Neave, a British forensic artist.

Once employed by the University of Manchester, Neave recovers faces, rebuilding them from the skull outwards. Of all the reconstructions of historical/ archaeological figures that he has done, his most famous work, in Greece, is the study of the father of Alexander the Great, Philippos II of Macedonia.

The skull of Vesalius is obviously the main prerequisite, if a reconstruction is to performed, and their first thought was that Vesalius's remains would obviously be entombed somewhere in Belgium. On doing research, however, they understood that Vesalius's grave was lost, and lying somewhere on the Greek Island of Zakynthos.

Pollier wrote to me soon after and told me of her dream: 'If we find his remains, we can create a full body reconstruction in bronze.' We could make a figure, she suggested, coming out of the sea onto the Laganas beach, lying half in the water, washed up, so to speak, while he contemplates a skull, a portrait of himself, that he is holding in his hand.

The dream of creating a reclining figure has changed over the months, and now has become a standing flay, stripped of his skin, still holding and contemplating a skull in his hand. Might this be his own lost skull?

There are hundreds of portraits of Andrea Vesalius in existence, but many of the artists took their artistic freedom very far indeed. In one image, he is depicted as a slim young man. He was indeed barely 28 years old when he wrote his masterpiece. In another painting he is portrayed as a wise, experienced individual, even though he already died at the age of fifty. Sometimes he is shown to have short, curly hair, in a particular picture with a well-groomed beard, in another image with a wild beard, sometimes short, sometimes long.

He is often shown to have red hair. Where does that come from? Pollier would say, 'cells that produce melanin', and as she went on to explain about one of her artworks, 'melanocyte' for these are responsible for creating the colour of the skin and hair. She is a redhead, but was Vesalius? It leaves one wondering whether the red hair was not used symbolically. Vesalius biographer Charles Donald O'Malley mentions in his standard work in 1964 the theory that red hair perhaps indicates a fiery temper, and a 'man of wrath'. In many portraits there is also a particular look, a rather broad back of the head, while his nose and various bumps on his forehead are also striking.

Just as often we look at supposed portraits of Vesalius, which are not of him at all.

A good example is that of Melchior von Brauweiler (1515–1569), a lawyer from Cologne, painted by Jan Steven van Calcar, which has been presented to us, over the years, as a portrait of Vesalius. In this painting there is a coat of arms that negates, absolutely, any connection with Vesalius.

Even the famous French biographer Henriette Chardac has the portrait of von Brauweiler representing Vesalius on the cover of her book, *Andreas Vesalius: Chirurgien des Rois (Surgeon of Kings)*. In March 2014, the Flemish magazine *Knack* illustrated a reference to our quest with the portrait of von Brauweiler. Even the prestigious American MIT, in their Pantheon project, listing the most prominent of this world, make the same mistake. Vesalius is represented also there by the German lawyer.

As far back as 1964, Theodoor Goddeeris explained to me, André Pecker, in his *Contribution à l' étude d'un tableau de Calcar (Contribution to the study of a painting of Calcar)*, put the blunder to rights, but it's not being picked up upon, and now I know why. When I asked MIT why Pecker's work, and also more recent evidence, is not taken into account, the answer came:

> 'We source all of our images from Wikimedia, since their Commons is a freely licensed media file repository. This (image) is provided by the Smithsonian. If this is indeed incorrect, you may want to consider contributing your domain knowledge to the Wikipedia article on Vesalius, and also adding your image (if there are no copyright issues). We can then follow up with the appropriate changes in Pantheon.'

It is clear that only a few 'mother portraits' have served as the source for the many. With, more or less, freedom to imitate, most portraits reflect the spirit of the times in which they were realized, rather than show what Vesalius actually looked like. Or they portray whatever activity Vesalius was involved in at any given time, for example, Vesalius the grave robber or Vesalius the imperial doctor. Or they depict him from wonder kid to wise old man, from devil to saint.

In fact, Vesalius approved only one portrait of himself. 'Then I no longer have to endure those that make me look worse than the epitome of the bad-tempered artist or wood cutter,' he once wrote. This 'approved' portrait is printed in his opus magnum.

To discover what Vesalius really looked, Pollier and Neave have to find his skull. They would not find this in Belgium, that much was soon clear to the BIOMAB team.

In the meantime, they have already done the exercise in the opposite direction; that is, they have worked from the outside inwards, and have poured a bronze bust of which one half of the head is a copy of the portrait in the *Fabrica* and the other half a face on which construction can be carried out. The real exercise will have to wait until we find his skull.

Pollier and Van de Velde travelled with the Belgian Medical Yachting Club, a group of sailing doctors, to the Ionian Islands, for the first time, in May 2010. The company of twenty or so Flemish doctors planned to make visits to the other Ionian islands and Patras.

Illus. 6: Portrait of Vesalius in his Fabrica, on plate II.

As they left the ladies on the docks of Zakynthos, the sailing doctors asked them, with a giggle, if they had not forgotten their buckets and spades. The ladies, meanwhile, had made arrangements to meet the Mayor and colleagues from the medical world and couldn't wait to visit the existing Vesalius monuments.

They discovered that the memorial to the alleged grave of Vesalius has disappeared. This came as a shock. The existence of a medieval well indicated to them that the monastery had once stood on this very spot. The magic of the place, however, grabbed the artists and bowled them over.

The scientific side of their nature was excited even more by fellow doctors at the hospital whom they later met. Immediately after their journey they sought support for their indignation at the Belgian School of Athens, and eventually came into contact with the Embassy of Belgium in Athens.

5. *Insula Vesalia*: Zakynthos, Greece

''Ill-come,' he said to him, 'to the Land of the Dead,
which we call *Insula Vesalia*.
Soon you, too, will follow our fate,
but you must not believe that we all pass with the rapidity granted by the grave.

From: *L'Isola del giorno prima* of Umberto Eco,
translated by William Weaver, 1995.

In a black suit, a tombstone tourist becomes a taphophile, otherwise known as a lover of funerary archeology. Given the (un)healthy attraction graves have for me, I gladly take the epithet as an honorary title: *taphos* in Greek is grave, and *philos* friend. So please call me a taphophile, a friend of graves.

All over the world, wherever I go, I spend more time in cemeteries than on beaches. This is not any different in Greece. The First Cemetery of Athens easily endures comparison with the Père Lachaise of Paris.

The cemetery of the port city of Piraeus, with Jewish, Catholic and Protestant graves, has also stolen my heart. As do the military cemeteries of the Commonwealth and the German army outside Athens, or the British fields of death on Kefalonia for example, or the Catholic resting fields on Syros. And what about Orthodox cemeteries?

They are always well taken care of. You'll often find beautiful marble statues, but it's clear that people do not like cemeteries. People are rather taphophobic today.

Everywhere along the Greek lanes you see chapels of remembrance dedicated to those who died at that place. Are these chapels becoming more important than graves?

After a while many even clean out the graves of their loved ones. The first grave is rented temporarily. This happens especially in the cities. After a few years, the family digs up the coffin and cleans the remains with wine, cheap cologne or expensive perfume. Bones are then interred in a family grave or in a metal box in an ossuary or bone gallery. Most, however, throw them into a common pit, to further decay. This is how they make their final farewell; with the spring-cleaning of the tomb, the grieving process ends.

A taphophile seeking graves, be it the famous Vesalius, or anybody elses, receives a pitiful look.

In Zakynthos all this is not too bad. Local poet and necromancer Zacharias Stoufis would undoubtedly agree with this, as his oeuvre with black verses and epitaphs, and written and photographed traces of death and remembrance, is much admired. Here they worship Romantic poets who were born on the island and died in exile; they know the verses by heart in which poets weep empty or lost graves. The mausoleums of Solomos and Kalvos are places of pilgrimage. Regular earthquakes, however, do not help to conserve gravestones. In many other places, history can easily be read and interpreted from them, but here, so many graves have been destroyed or looted.

While I walk through the history of Zakynthos at a trot, Greek friends would expect that I would pause longer than just this sentence about Homer who, in his Odysseus, called Zakynthos the woodland – not in this story!

They'd probably prefer to skip a chapter on the Fourth Crusade. But that I can't. To this very day, they curse the 'wrong' crusade of 1204, where, with the support of the Venetians, it was not Jerusalem that was freed from the Muslims, but Constantinople, as the capital of the Greek Byzantine Empire was plundered and made powerless.

During the Frankish period that followed, mainly French and Italian crusaders swarmed out as far as modern Greece, and that we can skip with difficulty. From the end of the 12th century it is the Orsinis, the Angevins of the House of Anjou and the Tocchis who rule Zakynthos. Here and there you can find their coat of arms on the island. Also the Franciscan monasteries that welcomed foreigners such as Vesalius date from that period.

In 1479 the Turks landed on the island and plundered the churches, including the monastery above the bay of Laganas, and the church of Santa Maria delle Grazie.

The Venetians then took the island again. They restored its character and its social classes. In 1628 the common people rebelled against the nobility and the bourgeoisie. Their sympathy for the rights of the French Revolution drove them into the arms of Napoleon, whose troops occupied the island in 1797. Barely a year later puts the Russian-Turkish fleet on the island and the restoration of the nobility takes place. As a semi-independent state we see this Ionian island, in the following decade, under the alternating control of the Turkish sultan, the Russian tsar and the French. On September 19, 1809, the British invade. They occupy the seven Ionian Islands that are unified with the Paris Agreement on November 5, 1815.

From here onwards, I'll behave as an ordinary taphophile again. When once I sent photos of a church with a graveyard to Pavlos Plessas to find out why I was so attracted to the place, it was found that the soil probably hid the very first English cemetery on the Island. And yet, so Plessas adds: 'around 1675 the British Consul fell out with the priest of this church and moved his cemetery to Ioanni Korae Street, around the corner from the dilapidated St John the Baptist Church in the city centre'.

In 1815, there was an English cemetery for British soldiers, next to the Catholic cemetery of St Mark. Both cemeteries are buried today under the open-air theatre of the town in Filikon Street. The tombstones were transferred to the cemetery of the Church of St John the Baptist.

Unfortunately a sign says: 'Beware. The cemetery is closed to the public, because of the danger of unstable monuments.' The chain to the iron gate could not stop me, however. I didn't need special permission as a sympathetic chat with the neighbour who takes care of the church gardens was equally effective. Reportedly there are plans to renovate the cemetery and open it to the public. I felt myself to be in the footsteps of the British Consul G. Sargint, who restored the cemetery in 1920, after previous repairs were made in 1821.

Consuls and their cemeteries: the story is not completely told.

From 1675 to 1870 it was mainly British soldiers who were buried in the British cemetery, but there were also a few missionaries, noble ladies and gentlemen, and the children and wives of those who were not welcome elsewhere.

There are also two English colleagues of mine: Clemens Harvey, Consul of the Peloponnese, died in 1689, and James Paul, Consul of Kefalonia and Zakynthos, died in 1728. I greet them with respect.

On the tombstone of Fredrick Dedrick, which is higher up, on the terrace, I read that he was the late Sergeant of the Band of the 11th Regiment of the British Infantry. He was born in a difficult-to-read city in Prussia in 1789 and died here on October 23, 1834. The stone was erected by his companions from the orchestra. Reading down from the top, below 'Sacred to the Memory of', stands the rudimentary but unmistakable image of the compasses and square. Masonic symbols and other public references to Freemasonry in the Ionian Islands are handled differently than in the rest of Greece. It is strange that many have such an aversion to a phenomenon that, in this country, is represented by the so-called 'regular masons' who are anything but atheist. And I may be wrong here, but doesn't it seem that the history of the country is being rewritten by downsizing the contribution of Freemasons to nation building? Not so in Zakynthos, although the resistance sometimes comes from an unexpected corner. On the Facebook page of Zacharias Stoufis, fellow gravedigger, I discover: 'As an island of masons, we have a surplus, we export.' So translated it sounds like confirmation that Freemasonry on Zakynthos is widely spread, so broad that many masons leave, even though I think Stoufis meant his statement to be taken as somewhat of a curse.

The first Freemason lodge in the region was opened in 1740 on Corfu 'Benefizenza', with the support of a lodge in Verona. 'La Philogenie', later renamed 'Saint Napoleon', since 1809 under the Grand Orient de France, appeared as a second one in 1807. On March 18, 1815, with the help of the Corfu lodges, 'the Resurrected Phoenix' was established on Zakynthos, which later transformed into the 'Star of the East', the only lodge in Greece which later falls directly under the United Grand Lodge of England.

Many of the masons of the islands, and of the rest of the country, have contributed a great deal to the struggle for independence. On Zakynthos lies the place that once hid one of the greatest secrets of the country. It is the cradle of the freedom struggle.

Just above the town, in the extension of Kapodistriou Street (Ioannis Kapodistrias first led the independent Greece) is Filikon Street (the Street of the Friends), which refers to the Society of Filiki Eteria, or the Friendly Society. Just past the open-air theatre which leads on to Psiloma, shortly after a sharp turn, is the church of Agios Georgis ton Filikon (St George of the Friends).

The steep street hides a path, halfway up, that leads, just after an apartment block to the right and a garden to the left, to a plateau. Behind the iron gate with the emblem of the Society of Filiki Eteria, shines, in bright red, a small, simple, rectangular church. At its eastern end, the visitor is welcomed by the bust of the austere hero of the Greek War of Independence, Theodoros Kolokotronis. Indeed, the man after whom the street where we situate Santa Maria delle Grazie is named.

At the northern end of the church, under the olive tree, stands the memorial stone of the secret Friendly Society. On its southern side, under the simple clock tower, is a birdcage-like mausoleum with weathered letters.

Against the side wall there is a memorial plaque, with square and compasses, to the masons who restored the church in 1953. To the west is the key on the door. No surprises in this church: the pews banked against the wall. A large silver-plated icon of St George with his horse rests on an easel. The iconostasis to the holiest is obviously closed. Among the lustre of the alternating black-and-white floor, there is a weathered grey stone with the double eagle of the Byzantine church.

An interesting discovery is a framed list of the Friends of the Secret Society, who from 1819 until 1821 were initiated here. In the lower right corner is the message that the original list, now in the Solomos Museum, was saved from the ruins by Nicolas Barbianis. In the alphabetical list of the last century are a few names that sound familiar, even today; Dionysios Barbianis for example, a forefather of the saviour, making them both, in their ways, heroes of history.

The turbulent years that followed have only recently reached the white screen of the cinema. From 2012 dates the film *God Loves Caviar*, the story of Ioannis Varvakis, pirate, caviar smuggler for Catherine (Deneuve) the Great, and hero of the revolution.

In Cinema Foscolos on Solomos Square, Zakynthos, I once read, to my surprise, in the credits: 'In 1825, the Greek War of Independence against the Ottoman Empire had been raging for three years. The Greek Civil War, directed by the great powers of that time, had just begun.' And then I saw how Varvakis is brought in to land in a boat, on 'the Greek island of Zakynthos under British dominion; sanatorium for infectious diseases'.

The sanatorium director (played by John Cleese), upon hearing who his prisoner is, chuckles: 'I did not know that age was contagious.' He adds: 'Honoured by the provisional government? As a benefactor of the country? And yet he is arrested. A dangerous benefactor then? Dangerous because he had dreams?'

In the final scene, I see that Varvakis died on Zakynthos in 1825. In the days and months that followed, I searched for, but did not find, his grave. Maybe he found his freedom elsewhere. Also in the heart of the Zakynthians?

The island would remain a while under the ruling of Britannia, but when the British recognized the independence of Greece, the islanders demanded their return to the mainland. This is what happened on May 21, 1864, which is in 2014 exactly 150 years ago.

During World War II, the Axis powers, the Italians and Germans, occupied the island. The neighbouring island of Kefalonia has a charming story and film as a remembrance of the times: *Captain Corelli's Mandolin* with Nicholas Cage and Penelope Cruz, from the book by Louis de Bernières.

Zakynthos will, one day, get its film about World War II. During one of my visits, a film crew explored the island with a view to film the story of the miraculous rescue of the island's Jews during World War II. The governor of the German occupation, in September 1943, asked the mayor, Loukas Karrer, for a list of all the Jews on the island. The following day, the mayor and the bishop Chrysostomos, handed over two names only: their own. In October 1944, when the Germans retreated, 275 Jews of Zakynthos remained alive; this was different from the sad reality of the rest of the country.

The Jewish cemetery is one of my favorite places to meditate on the island. In the alley to the Church of St George of the Friends, which is hard to find on a first visit, is a barely visible Star of David above a doorway to a derelict garden. Hidden behind the hedge is a pair of snow-white marble memorial slabs. On each visit another memorial is added. Only later did I see, on the top of the terraces, hundreds of graves, weathered, from simple to richly adorned; some of them are said to go back to 1545, decades before Vesalius landed on the island.

6. Vesalius in the Pantheon

Sailing doctors surely know what *des vents contraires* are. Headwinds, I translate spontaneously, although that sounds as though it should be 'dead winds' in English, which sounds so much nicer. Winds that kill, but in what way?

There have been reams of paper and as many bits and bytes wasted on hypotheses about the death of Vesalius. Did he perish in a shipwreck as stormy deadwinds blew? Did he die of scurvy because he was on a journey that took too long, in the dearth of wind? Did the wind come from the wrong direction or was there no wind at all?

Vesalius was thrown on Zakynthos by *des vents contraires*. Thus, with great self-assurance, says the commemorative medal from 1846 designed by Christian Adolphe Jouvenel, 'engraver of royal medals', - 'Belgian School', adds Maurits Biesbrouck in his study: 'Andreas Vesalius in nummis'.

I received the medal as a gift from Jan Driessen. Later, after our reconnaissance trip that I mentioned in the introduction, he gave me a second medal as a souvenir. That copy is larger and heavier, has more bas relief and carries on the reverse a representation of the *Fabrica* of Vesalius and the title that was missing on the first medal, '*Vésale que Bruxelles a vu naître...*' (*Vesalius known to be born in Brussels*).

With the founding of Belgium in 1830, parliament went looking for an identity. The young nation, surrounded by powerful neighbours, had to have an equally prestigious past. Thus it searched for Belgians who were known around the world. Vesalius was at the top of the list. Our representatives felt that the Brussels-born doctor, who is regarded worldwide as the father of human anatomy, best fulfilled this Belgian ambition. In those early years of the new Belgium, no expense was spared to 'make' him: most busts, statues and other memorabilia date from the 19th century.

As I write this, a young Vesalius, with a long beard, looks down on me. The bust was created by an artist from Mechelen, Joseph Willems, for the legendary Brussels foundry, the Compagnie des Bronzes. From 1853 to 1977, the company produced industrial objects in bronze and zinc and became internationally renowned for its art and decorative works. Foundry worker and artist Luc De Blick, who since 1972 had worked as mouldmaker and engraver, rescued from the company's bankruptcy dozens of moulds that the foundry did not donate to the Museum of Industrial Archaeology, because they were not considered to be interesting enough. The mould of Vesalius's bust then moved from Brussels to Glabbeek, where in the eighties Luc de Blick had poured a pair of bronze copies. Today my family greets the sculpture with its brown patina with a lot of irony.

For years the Leuven Vesalius specialists, Omer Steeno, Maurice Biesbrouck and Theodoor Goddeeris, have been identifying and describing Vesalius memorabilia. Their articles are gems and tell tales of unknown stories.

A medal on eBay, a picture offered by an auction house, a facsimile of the *Fabrica* for a bargain or, if you wish, an original *Fabrica* 1543 issued by Oporinus for a quarter of a million euro? For a tip about any Vesalius memorabilia on the market, you have to check with them.

From the 19th century until today Vesalius is regarded as one of the greatest of Belgium and beyond. The Macro Connections Group at MIT's Media Lab launched the Pantheon project and, despite being illustrated with an incorrect picture, Vesalius holds 1,105th place in a list of 7,757 world celebrities. He has a Wikipedia page in 49 different languages and since 2008, a total of 2,610,011 visits. He is the 12th of 146 doctors, the first of three contemporary doctors and 11th of 500 Belgians. (According to this Pantheon database Charles V, the employer of Vesalius, is fourth on the list of our most famous countrymen.)

In 2002, the BBC created a TV programme that went in search of the One Hundred Greatest Britons. In 2005, the idea was repeated in our country. Both Flemish and Canvas Radio 1, as well as the French-speaking RTBF, engaged in the exercise and went looking for the Greatest Belgian. The ranking was not the same in both parts the country.

In Flanders, Andreas Vesalius was sixth, after Adolf Daens, Ambiorix, Eddy Merckx, Paul Janssens and the winner, Father Damien. The case for Vesalius was presented by Robrecht Van Hee, Antwerp professor of history of medicine.

In Wallonia, Jacques Brel was chosen, Father Damien was in third place, cyclist Merckx in fourth and Andreas Vesalius in nineteenth place.

As coordinator of the Belgian Vesalius activities in Greece for the ad hoc group Vesalius Continuum, I noticed that there is a big difference in how the two communities prepare to celebrate the 500ᵗʰ anniversary of the birth of Vesalius.

The French and Brussels communities seem to show less interest in the Vesalius celebrations. The internationally renowned Vesalius College of the Vrije Universiteit Brussel ordered, a few years ago, a new bust of its 'patron saint' but regarding the celebrations of his birthday, I don't hear much at all. The dean of the institute would like to organize something, but because the institute doesn't offer medicine or natural sciences, he feels that there is no obvious line of approach for him to take.

The Brussels Rotary Club Vésale, which carries three weasels in their newsletter, once sent me some photos of their visit to Zakynthos, but that was as far as it went.

My old contact in the Atheneum, Robert Catteau, referred me to the alumni association, but that also faded out. Maybe some initiatives here and there will still develop.

In Flanders, it is different. Antwerp and Leuven are competing for attention. In Antwerp, the Lambotte museum and the Plantin – Moretus Museum host exhibitions and the University organizes lectures and more. In Leuven, a joint committee is coordinating an exhibition at the M-Museum, lectures in the Gasthuisberg hospital, striking medals, and city walks by the tourist office to places that remind us of Vesalius. The Anatomical Theatre, which has recently been renovated, is once again open to the public. There is also a first publication in facsimile of the new Dutch translation of the *Fabrica* by Maurits Biesbrouck.

Particularly noticeable is the fact that the institutions of the Flemish government are just a bit lukewarm in their Vesalius interest. To say that the Flemish Community is losing interest in a world famous Flemish-speaking 'Brusselaar' is, I suppose, exaggerated.

The Federal Belgium reacts in a different way. As with previous celebrations the Belgian post office is introducing a new Vesalius stamp. The Federal Public Service of Foreign Affairs, dreaming aloud of economic diplomacy, is introducing Andreas Vesalius as a trump card to help promote Belgian business abroad. A colleague of mine who has an eye for economic spin wishes to use the image of Vesalius as a shining example of how our country is still a powerful force in the medical and pharmaceutical field.

The Embassy of Belgium in Athens receives from the Home Office all the support that it asks for, despite cutbacks. With Marc Van den Reeck, Ambassador of Belgium in Greece, we had already launched a new concept in Athens and the rest of Greece, under the name *Ta Velgika* – Things from Belgium, preceding the suggestion of the colleagues in Brussels dealing with the Belgian image abroad. The company that was the first to enthusiastically respond to a request for cooperation in the Vesalius project is the world leader in the field of medical imaging, Agfa HealthCare, the Greek branch of Agfa Gevaert. They are sponsoring a digital map of the area where we situate the Santa Maria with the cemetery in which we think Vesalius is buried.

The Embassy of Belgium in Riga is collaborating with the Pauls Stradiņš Museum of the History of Medicine for an exhibition entitled 'The Anatomist, the Fabric of the Human Body'. Among the exhibited items is a digitalized version of the second edition of the *Humani Corporis Fabrica*, together with specimens of the anatomical collection of the museum, displayed in a modern setting. The museum has in its possession a copy of the painting of Vesalius by the Ostend painter E.J. Hamman.

Simultaneously the Embassy will organize a competition for Latvian cartoonists. Also the exhibition 'Fabrica Vitae', curated by Eleanor Crook and Pascale Pollier, will travel to the Pauls Stradiņš Museum. Named after the most prominent doctor of Latvia, the museum is one of the largest of its kind in the world. The Embassy of Belgium was one of the former occupiers of the majestic building at this address: Antonijas iela 1. Ambassador Frank Arnauts and Director Juris Salaks meet regularly, as Omer Steeno corresponds with both of them.

The Embassy of Belgium in Copenhagen is planning festivities with a scientific symposium, together with the department of neuroscience and pharmacology (PANUM institute of the University of Copenhagen), and Professor Ron Kupers, coordinator of the BRAINlab. The occasion is also the 64th session of the European Regional Committee of the World Health Organization (WHO).

The pinnacle of the celebration will take place on Zakynthos. Where Andreas Vesalius died 450 years ago, an international conference, a new monument, a contemporary art exhibition, film screenings and concerts will build bridges between here and there, between yesterday and tomorrow. Vesalius Continuum.

7. The grave of Belgium's honoured son

> You, Grand benefactor of humanity
> and honoured child of Belgium
> who were thrown from the tide of life
> to the angry wave of the sea.
>
> To the Greek seacoast fate forsook you
> in the blue colour of our sky.
> And as an affectionate mother sweetly covered you
> the fragrant soil of Zakynthos.
>
> From 'To the great Belgian anatomist
> Andreas Vesalius', 1964,
> by Crysanthi Zitsaia.

Seeking an identity for his country, the first ruler of the new Belgium, King Leopold I, asked for more information about the tomb of Vesalius very soon after independence. According to Omer Steeno the king was responding to the suggestion of A. Burggraeve, Professor of Anatomy at the University of Ghent, who formulated this request in his book on Vesalius in 1841.

How the King would have asked this 'through his government' is not clear. From government to government? Through diplomatic channels, I wonder?

Our country opened a diplomatic mission in Athens eight years after our independence, successively represented by: Benjamin Mary (from 1838), C. Rodenbach (from 1846) and J. Vermeersch (from 1847).

In 1861 the Consulate General was opened, the head of which was Baron de Streil. From 1869 until the arrival of Baron Guillaume in 1894, Belgium had no representative. If the King's request for more information ran via Athens and through diplomatic channels, it happened between 1841 and 1869. But to whom was the question addressed?

In his book, *Vesalius and the Evolution of Anatomy*, published in 1953, Greek historian Nicolas Barbianis seemed to be sure that the question was addressed to the 'Western Church', meaning the Catholic Diocese. I quote the complete excerpt from the booklet of Barbianis because his 'aside' thoughts are really worth reading:

'The Belgian Government has, through a document intended for the Western Diocese of Zakynthos, requested relevant information about Vesalius, perhaps because the Kingdom was planning to repatriate the bones of its famous son to Belgium. The circumstances at the time, however, including destruction, earthquakes, fire, looting, successive changes of state, etc. made it difficult and unfortunately none of these events showed specific tracks or clues about the tomb of the great Belgian anatomist. The archives of the Western Diocese reportedly remain silent on this. According to (local historian) Leonidas Zois, however, a thorough examination and a study of the extensive archives of the Saint Marco church, the old church for Catholics in Zakynthos, is highly recommended. This archive was hitherto not classified, not studied and was unpublished.'

I consulted with Prof. Gustaaf Jansens, Archivist of the Royal Palace, but as Steeno had experienced earlier, nothing was found there.

Also on Steeno's sugggestion I approached Spiros Gaoutsis, colleague and Honorary Consul of Malta to Corfu, and Secretary of Ioannis Spiteris, Catholic Archbishop of Corfu, Zakynthos and Kefalonia, who resides in Corfu today. In his message, Gaoutsis explains that the German Air Force bombed Corfu in September 1943. Archives that were not lost then were destroyed ten years later, when the great earthquake hit the region and all historical sources, libraries and archives went up in smoke. He even looked in Rome, but there too he found nothing about those first initiatives of trying to locate the grave in the Santa Maria.

Until something turns up, we must assume that the Embassy in the early days of our country could report little or nothing to the King about the grave of Vesalius. The conditions were not helpful, as Nicolas Barbianis acknowledged. The Greek War of Independence in 1864 reached Zakynthos; from 1869 to 1894 we had no envoy in Greece; and in 1893 an earthquake destroyed the island, again, and not for the last time.

In the confusing years that followed, we heard little from the Belgian representatives in Athens about Vesalius. If I still list their names it is just for the sound of it. Until 1903 the following sat in the ambassador's chair in Athens: Baron Guillaume, followed by Baron de Groote, Baron de Gaiffier d'Hestroy, M. Sainctelette and Prince de Caraman-Chimay.

That list says more about the nature of Belgian diplomacy in those years than about any interest in Vesalius. But that interest was soon to come, as well as a change in diplomacy.

On March 12, 1911, and until the arrival of the Count G. Errembault Dudzeele on September 30, 1916, J. Mélot was the representative of our country in Greece. In the run up to the big Vesalius Celebration in 1914, four hundred years after his birth, Mélot undoubtedly corresponded with compatriot and Belgian professor Jean-Joseph Tricot-Royer.

From different sources, we hear that Tricot-Royer in those years did indeed have plans for a Vesalius birthday commemoration. Specifically, he wanted to create a commemorative plaque on Zakynthos. He announced this intention in a speech at the Sorbonne on April 2, 1914. The world-renowned medical journal *The Lancet* reveals in its 1914 issue (1:1198) that he wanted to unveil the monument in August of that year. In 1966, more than fifty years later, in the *Dutch Journal of Dentistry*, more details on the monument he planned to erect came to light; for example: 'The design was created by engraver Edouard Pellens and a beautiful text was written by a priest of Mechelen, named Van Caster. The Belgian government supported the initiative. Unfortunately, World War I broke the momentum and everything would have to be redone.'

War already rumbled in Europe when the Belgian professor was making his plans in Paris, and in early August 1914, Germany indeed declared war on our country. Travelling abroad was not possible for several years.

Whether or not Tricot-Royer corresponded with the embassy is not yet clear. Whether or not he made or even planned a trip to Zakynthos will hopefully become clear soon. This year, the grandson of Tricot-Royer, Jean-Pierre Tricot hopes to republish the booklet of his grandfather, *Vie de Vésale*. Jean-Pierre Tricot was previously president of the International Association for the History of Medicine, which was founded by his grandfather. He himself founded *Vesalius,* the journal of the association.

Naturally, I asked him about his grandfather. I was surprised to read in his e-mail of July 30, 2012, that his grandfather 'had undertaken a trip to Zakynthos in search of the grave (in which he was unsuccessful)'.

An aside: Vesalius as a historical figure has evoked a passionate reaction over generations of entire families. One of the families inspired by the anatomist is father and son Ladikos, in Zakynthos. The Antwerp Tricot family passes on Vesalius's legacy from grandfather to grandson.

I tried for a while also to find out more about the connection between the priest from Mechelen and the commemorative plaque, but I unfortunately stalled. Obviously François van der Jeught, Secretary of the Royal Society for Archaeology, Literature and Art of Mechelen, knows of the former president of his Society, Priest William Van Caster. He put me in touch with the former secretary, who published a short biography of Van Caster, but it doesn't contain any references to the commemorative plaque. The priest was known for numerous inscriptions (including commemorative verses). Edward Pellens was also rather well known for his illustrations, which appeared on stamps.

From the article 'Memories of and tributes to Andreas Vesalius on the Ionian island of Zakynthos (Zante)' by Omer Steeno, I note that during the following years, between the two world wars, other attempts to find the grave were made by the local scholar Spiro de Biasi in 1919 and the Italian historian Dr. Pietro Capparoni in 1923.

They focused on the Santa Maria delle Grazie Church, and reported that 'the church was destroyed in the mid-19th century by an earthquake. Rebuilt, it was again destroyed in 1893 and the building stones were re-used in the construction of the homes of the fishermen living on the coast.

The archives of the church were transferred to Athens in 1983. We also know that the parish registers of Zakynthos began in 1590 and that the city archives were destroyed during the fire of 1612.' Here endeth the statement of Omer Steeno.

Dr. G.J.M. (Gert Jan) van Wijngaarden, the Dutch archaeologist who has been searching for a temple of Artemis on Zakynthos since 2005 for the University of Amsterdam, adds in an e-mail: 'During the building of the Santa Maria Church in 1544, tombstones were found that made reference to Cicero. The church was later expanded and became a monastery, later a hospital and then a barracks.'

The barracks were initially occupied by the British Army and later the Greek Army, specifies Nicolas Barbianis. 'In 1944, the building was destroyed by the Italian/German Army,' concludes van Wijngaarden.

In 1956, Georges Sarton, an internationally acclaimed scientist from Cambridge, USA, (originally born in Ghent on August 30, 1884) passed away. In 1914 he had fled to London, soon crossed the ocean to the U.S. and then taught at Harvard from 1916 onwards. He is best known for a five-part *Introduction to the History of Science* (1936), and as the founder of the scientific journals *Isis* (1912) and *Osiris* (1936). In 1954, an article was published in *Isis* with a title that sounds more ironic than was intended: 'The death and burial of Vesalius, and, incidentally, of Cicero.'

Sarton, unfortunately somewhat forgotten in our country, is undeniably one of us. I understand that the author mainly wants to talk about Vesalius, but cannot ignore the fate of the Roman orator. On the other hand, the title suggests that the death and funeral of Vesalius are more important than the death of Cicero, and that, of course, we understand very well.

In his introduction, Sarton continues that his friend Professor Michael Stephanides of the University of Athens presented him with the study of Nicolas Barbianis. In his article, Sarton elaborated upon this information, with personal additions: 'Stumbling upon Cicero whilst hunting for Vesalius is so strange that I have to tell it even if that story is not relevant here,' so I quote him literally. Cicero was murdered by agents of Mark Antony on December 7, 43 BC. His head and right hand were taken to Rome. It is said that the rest of his body, or his ashes, were taken to Zakynthos by a slave or by his son

The tomb of Cicero (or what people thought was his tomb) was discovered in 1544, when the foundations of a monastery were laid and he was reburied in the Santa Maria delle Grazie. In 1556 in Venice or Padua a paper was published describing the discovery of the tomb, and made reference to a drawing of the tombstone, an urn of ashes, a bottle of tears and the epitaph, so Sarton says:

M. CICERO TYLLI HAVE. ET. TV TERTIA ANTONIA
Hail Marcus Tullius Cicero and you Antonia the third

The grave must have existed, but did it really contain the remains of Cicero and his wife Antonia Tertia? Could it have been the remains of his son and his mother?

Maurice Biesbrouck discovered an almost identical reference to the grave in the work of Olfert Dapper (1688), with the following addition: 'The front part of the tomb was subsequently brought to Venice, to the home of Federico Contarini, a lover of antiquities, who conserved the stone for a very long time.' Here endeth a casual reference to the lost grave of Cicero in the Santa Maria delle Grazie.

8. The anatomist and the pharmacist

The ashes and bones of Vesalius, sacred to the world,
whoever finds them on this isolated island,
passing by the wild shores of
the woodland that is Zakynthos,
should hold his tired steps,
and believe that it is here
that Vesalius met the ultimate goal of nature
and understood that striving for anything else
is pointless

free translation of the epigram on Vesalius's grave,
as quoted by N. Barbianis,
in *Signs of Death, Belief and Memory
in the streets of Zakynthos* by Zacharias Stoufis, 1990.

If Andreas Vesalius, who does not have a known grave on Zakynthos, still lives there, in the hearts of the islanders, it is, indeed, first and foremost thanks to Nicolas Barbianis, who also advised Sarton.

This sentence is hardly intended to be ambiguous. The fact is that history is written by discoveries that overtake each other, and when this happens, new hypotheses do not diminish the merits of previous researchers.

On Zakynthos, the names of Vesalius and Barbianis will remain forever linked, and if it were up to me, for more than sixty years. During the Vesalius Continuum Conference, Katerina Demeti, Director of the Solomos and Kalvos museum, will honour Barbianis with a paper about his legacy.

In 1962, Belgium honoured Nicolas Barbianis for his commitment. On June 7 of that year, the then Ambassador, Geoffroy d'Aspremont Lynden, pinned on his chest the medal of Officer of the Order of Leopold II, during a reception at the Chancery of the Embassy in Athens. In a report to then Minister of Foreign Affairs, Paul-Henri Spaak, the Ambassador wrote that Barbianis was particularly sensitive to the honour that was bestowed upon him. The acclaimed researcher asked the Ambassador to pass on his gratitude to the King and the Belgian parliament and to assure them of his continued dedication to 'the cause of Andreas Vesalius'.

A month later, on July 9, 1962, the Ambassador reported to his minister that the mayor of Zakynthos, M.J. Margaris, thanked our country 'for the honour that it manifests to Barbianis, which in turn is reflected on the entire island. The efforts of this tireless man of letters show precisely how generous and free Zante feels towards Belgium.'

Nicolas Barbianis has worked, since the forties, for the 'Andreas Vesalius cause' and he will continue to persevere tirelessly until his death.

In July 1953 he published the book, *The Evolution of Anatomy and Andreas Vesalius*, with a short summary in French and a foreword by the president of the prestigious Academy of Sciences and Fine Arts of Athens.

After an outline of the history of human anatomy, with great attention given to the Greek classical past in that area, and following several chapters on the life and work of Vesalius, the fourth part is devoted to 'the problem of the precise location of the grave'.

Here the author puts forward his findings as he had announced them a year earlier. On April 3, 1952, at the Academy of Athens, he had presented his findings in a communication entitled 'The place in Zakynthos where the great anatomist Andreas Vesalius died and was buried'. I quote from the French summary a telling piece about the sources of Barbianis's work:

> 'His research work involves reading the works of foreign travelers and historians, but is based primarily on interviews with local sources, ancient folk traditions and personal archaeological research.'

Thanks to a translation into Dutch, by a Greek student commissioned by Omer Steeno, then revised by Maurice Biesbrouck, I was able to get, from the booklet of Barbianis, an excellent overview of the two main hypotheses about the location of the grave, as they were known then.

Particularly striking is the detailed and convincing list of sources advocating the Santa Maria delle Grazie Church theory. And then Nicolas Barbianis quotes from the chronicles of Dion. (Dionysios) Barbianis (1788–1866), whom we earlier encountered in the Church of St George of the Friends (on the list of the initiated heroes of the War of Independence).

I was struck by one particular sentence: 'it is rather unusual that the location where this precious monument was, is not known.'

Later Pavlos Plessas told me that Greek historian Dinos Konomos dedicated almost three pages to explaining the full meaning of this sentence. According to Konomos, Dionysios Barbianis didn't write the sentence at all and it was added by Nicolas Barbianis.

In fact ancestor Barbianis had copied the *unpublished* translation, by the Zakynthian writer Nicolaos Serras, of a book of the Catholic Bishop of Kefalonia/ Zakynthos, Balthassare Maria Remondine. It was Nicolaos Serras himself who said that he had made many corrections and additions in his translation of the book of the bishop. One of the additions was a clear reference to the grave of Vesalius in the Santa Maria delle Grazie. The manuscript of Dionysios Barbianis was unfortunately lost during the earthquake of 1953. A few months earlier, however, the pages of the copied translation of Serras had already been found to be missing. In another copy, later discovered by Ifigeneia Anastasiadou in Venice, and in a translation of the work of Serras by the local historian Leonidas H. Zois, however, the disputed sentence does not appear.

Here endeth the analyses of Dinos Konomos (in a synopsis of the translation by Pavlos Plessas), who concludes that Nicolas Barbianis wrote the sentence himself.

Nonetheless, it had already occurred to me that Nicolas Barbianis's thesis is built upon this one sentence, because he goes on to say: 'Dionysios Barbianis's doubts about the Santa Maria are reinforced by the word of mouth of the elders of the area of Laganas, which we have documented.' Based upon the authority of forefather Dionysios, Nicolas went looking for the grave elsewhere, in Laganas.

Laganas is in the bay of the same name, in the area called Frankoklisi, referring to a Frankish church. The construction of this church by Franciscan monks is dated from the year 1216, when all over Greece similar Frankish churches and monasteries were founded; one of my frequent destinations, indeed, is the ruins of such a Frankoklisi, on the Mountain of Pendelis, which I can see from my window. Quite why Nicolas Barbianis was so determined to search for the grave in this particular place is unclear.

The fact that there is no concrete evidence to prove that there is a grave in the Santa Maria delle Grazie in the city centre, as he claimed earlier, is not an argument, because there isn't any evidence in existence that suggests the grave is to be found at this chosen location in the countryside either.

Admittedly, this place continues to intrigue many to this day. If Nicolas Barbianis in his search and hard work had merely kept the memory of Vesalius alive, that would be more than enough, but documenting the collective memory of that neighbourhood was a timeless contribution too. In any case I really enjoy the stories he and his team of researchers have collected.

According to Barbianis, the supposed tomb of Vesalius was visited by priests from Malta and English tourists on horseback from the town of Zakynthos. But he also says that of the Frankoklisi almost nothing remains. From local residents, he notes that a few years ago ruins of the Western Church of the Holy Theodoors (there were indeed two of them) were visible, including the foundations of many buildings, remains of a lime kiln, textile fabrics and a large stone well, which we will stumble upon later in this saga.

One of the former tenants of the land, which was leased from the Catholic Church in the city, notes that his old father had found there a stone that carried a carved out cross and an unreadable text. Overnight he had hidden the stone with the intention to donate it to the Orthodox Church in his village as an altarpiece. Sad to say, the stone was stolen that very same night by neighbours who used it in the construction of a building.

The former owner also told Barbianis that 'until recently, excavated human skeletons were regularly discovered, some of them in a sitting position, within vaulted tombs, and one with a sword next to it. Foundations of tall buildings, fragments of roof tiles and ancient clay pots also occasionally came to light.' But everything that was found, Barbianis continues, was re-used as building material by the local residents, for their houses. He himself had seen stones with 'faded inscriptions, crosses and half-erased lines of foreign words', which screamed out for further research.

It is particularly striking that in his article Barbianis yet again formulates doubts about the cause of death of Vesalius. It is inconceivable to him that Vesalius had been abandoned by the 'inhospitable islanders' or by the then well-organized Venetian government on the island. Thus he slowly slips back into the thought process of the second hypothesis, which says that Vesalius was buried within the Catholic city church. In a very detailed conclusion, he states that all useful documentation about Vesalius had either been destroyed or still lay hidden somewhere in an archive.

To give his hypothetical research a material form, Barbianis suggested to the Prefect of Zante, Demetris Sambatakakis, that a monument should be inaugurated, not in the city centre. It was unveiled at the mythical place near Laganas that is called Kalogerata today, in 1952. From the old photographs that exist, I cannot determine how large the memorial was exactly; there was nothing to compare it with. I would guess it was about fifty centimetres wide and a metre and a half high. At the top, in the centre, there is a cross, decorated on either side with carved ribbons, which run down the whole length of the carved emblem, and taper towards the foot of the cross. In the middle of the stone is a metal plate and inlaid in Greek are the words:

Here was the Franciscan Monastery
Holy Theodoors
Kalogerata
1471
where on the deserted beach
washed ashore
the body of the great anatomist
Andreas Vesalius
1564

I understand why Barbianis felt so attracted to this place. It offers even today 'a wonderful view: the big open sea allows the viewer's eye to stretch from side to side and far into the horizon. Here an impressive silence causes an almost religious delight.' The hill is today an ancient olive grove and sporadic cypresses reinforce the sacred aura. The medieval well still intrigues, but as Pollier and Van de Velde observed, the headstone mounted here by Barbianis has disappeared. Stolen in the same place from where the legendary stone with strange characters, meant to serve as an altar in a church, had previously disappeared. The Barbianis stone, though, probably belongs in a more diabolical scenario than the altar stone, as I will show later.

Illus. 7: Old photograph of the lost Barbianis Monument in Kalogerata.

In his booklet of 1953, Barbianis proudly announced that in a year's time he would unveil a new bust of Vesalius in the town of Zakynthos – to be precise, in April 1954, on the occasion of the 10th Medical Congress of the Medical Society of Athens. He had been in correspondence with the Ambassador of Belgium in Athens, Remi Baert. In their response, the society even dreams of an international conference, also on Zakynthos.

Finally in 2014, his dream will have come true when Ambassador Van den Reeck reveals the monument that Pascale Pollier, Richard Neave and Chantal Pollier have created.

In the very fruitful years of 1952 and 1953 Barbianis corresponded intensively with the Belgian government and other international contacts. For example, he regularly and proudly refers to contacts he has made with prominent scholars in the United States. One of his correspondents in Belgium is Gustaaf van der Schueren, Professor of Anatomy at the University of Leuven.

A further aside: after father and son Ladikos, after grandfather and grandson Tricot (-Royer), we have the granddaughter of Gustaaf van der Schueren, who happens to have been one of the students of the Sacred Heart Institute Heverlee that visited Zakynthos in 2014. Furthermore, the daughter of Katerina Demeti, granddaughter of Ioannis Demetis, who directed the Solomos Museum over two generations, would have travelled in the same school exchange to Leuven. There should be no doubt: Vesalius is not only contagious – his virus is so resistant that it survives generations.

From the archives of Gustaaf van der Schueren, Omer Steeno has unearthed a treasure chest of letters. Some of these show that Barbianis was trying to gain interest in his plans from Monseigneur H. Van Waeyenbergh, the Rector of the University of Leuven. In another letter it appears that the Counsellor of the Belgian Embassy, Borel de Bitche, checked out with the very same university, the information he received from Barbianis. It is, however, his boss, the Ambassador of Belgium, who was to receive the answer from the university. Finally, Remi Baert was to put all the parts together in a report to Paul Van Zeeland, then Minister of Foreign Affairs, in July 1953.

The Ambassador makes a mistake, however, when he puts forward the common proposals of Barbianis, Van der Schueren and the medical society as initiatives to commemorate the 400th anniversary of Vesalius. Was he mistaken in 1953 by half a century (1514-1914), or just ten years (1564-1964)?

The Ambassador proves again that he really does not like numbers. The paragraphs that follow in that same letter give me déjà vu as we today commemorate the 450th year of his death, 500 years since his birth in Brussels.

Ambassador Baert had been approached to co-sponsor a monument, a bust of Vesalius, the cost of which was not clear to him. For the bust, the Medical Society asked half a million Belgian francs (Bef), but could contribute 25,000 Bef themselves.

Conferences of the fifties and today do not differ a great deal where sponsoring is concerned.

9. ... or vice versa

> no more, no more upon thy verdant slopes!
> No more! alas, that magical sad sound transforming all!
>
> from 'Sonnet to Zante' (1837) by Edgar Allan Poe,
> carved onto a column on the estate of Nikos Varvianis

On August 12, 1953, Zakynthos and the neighbouring islands of Kefalonia and Ithaka were struck by their fate.

On that Wednesday, around noon, an earthquake caused the pointer on the Richter scale to fall beyond the seven mark. Despite the warnings of the recent days, since the previous Sunday in fact, of shaking and tremors as the plates in the ground moved against each other, and despite the midday attack, there were hundreds of victims. The worst hit was Zakynthos town which was razed to the ground. Almost all the buildings collapsed; the fires did the rest.

Barbianis was standing in the laboratory of his pharmacy when it began. He had just got out of the house and as a friend later noted: 'He saw the city die. Dust filled the air. It was getting dark and deadly silent.' In the following hours and days Barbianis contributed to the care of victims and later saved all kinds of treasures from the buildings. For weeks, he assembled dozens of thick albums with photographs, sketches and notes of his work. The grandson of Nicolas Barbianis, Nikos Varvianis, who preserves most of the albums carefully, has shown them to me: haunting witness reports that leave nobody unaffected. Browsing and reading the reports is painful. They should be published one day, exactly as they are. Just as the images I saw a few months ago on Greek television of the devastation caused by the earthquakes in Kefalonia, so the albums of Barbianis give me a real image of Zakynthos in 1953.

The Solomos and Kalvos Museum of Zakynthos also has such an album and many more artefacts and records that Barbianis saved.

It is very important for the whole of Greece that in 1953 Barbianis also took part in saving some of the manuscripts of Dionysios Solomos that were kept on Zakynthos. Born and raised on the island, Solomos is the author of the national anthem of Greece. The manuscripts of Solomos today are spread over several sites and published in facsimile, with a word of thanks to the man who helped save them, Nicolas Barbianis.

As the list of initiates in the church of St George of the Friends suggests, he also saved the archives of the Masonic Lodge, The Star of the East, which has accumulated to date more than one hundred and fifty years of continuous activity. In a letter to the rector of the University of Leuven, Barbianis had earlier written that he had given a speech on Vesalius in the public hall of the lodge. That hall is today named after Nicolas Barbianis.

Barbianis continued to work tirelessly for the cause of Andreas Vesalius. On December 11, 1960, the square to the new city library is officially named as the Vesalius Square.

The Belgian ambassador Count d'Aspremont-Lyden, and N. Martacos, the Consul, travel from Athens to Zakynthos. A week later, on December 16, 1960, the Ambassador reported on his visit to Zakynthos.

This diplomatic report from a French-speaking nobleman telling of his encounter with 'a good farmer, two constables, a young shepherd, and some villagers' is more than half a century old. We forgive the Ambassador for a somewhat paternalistic tone. I fear that he, like so many before him, and so many after him, had lost his heart here. The moving scene of receiving a handful of wild flowers, a jar of jam and a glass of fresh well water had brought him into a bucolic mood.

Count Geoffroy d'Aspremont Lynden
Ambassador of Belgium in Athens
to
Mr Pierre Wigny
Minister of Foreign Affairs
Brussels

Fourteen days ago I received a letter from the mayor of Zakynthos. He invited me to inaugurate the naming of the new square after Andreas Vesalius.

It is one of the main squares of the city and was rebuilt after the terrible earthquake and fires of 1953. The city insisted that the new square should be named in honour of the great Belgian anatomist.

Despite the bad weather and the close proximity of the large ball that I am to organize on the occasion of the marriage of our King [Baldwin], I felt that the invitation was so flattering for our country I could not refuse.

In the company of the Consul Martacos, I took a regular ship in Piraeus. On Saturday, December 10, the ferries between the coast of Zante and the Peleponnesos did not sail because of a storm. On Sunday morning, however, at five o'clock, we arrived on the island.

Despite the early hour, we were met on the dock and welcomed by the Prefect, the Mayor and Mr Barbianis, one of the notables of the island. The latter is passionately looking for the grave of our illustrious countryman. He has a well-received brochure published about the work and the circumstances of Vesalius's death, which he presented at the Academy of Athens.

After courtesy visits to the Orthodox Metropolitan, on the previous day, the Prefect and the Mayor and I laid a laurel wreath at the War Memorial that had a ribbon in our tricolor and in Greek the following text: 'Commissioned by the Embassy of Belgium for all the heroes who died for the Fatherland'. The local authorities attended the ceremony, which was brought to a close by the national anthems of our countries, brilliantly played by the local brass band, and to a large audience.

After that, everyone marched on foot to the square that was to be dedicated to Andreas Vesalius. The Metropolitan and Catholic priests had joined the officials. The ceremony was opened with a speech by the Mayor followed by a eulogy in French by the President of the Medical Association.

I replied with an address in Greek, which you will find attached with a translation into French. I insisted on speaking in Greek because I know that such an effort is always greatly appreciated by both the government and the public. I must tell you that the residents did not spare their applause and cheers. To the sound of 'Hail, Hail, O freedom', the Greek National anthem, whose lyrics were written by the great poet Solomos who was born on the island, and the national anthem of Belgium, I unveiled the plaque to Andreas Vesalius by the dropping of the tapestry which had echoes of the Greek and Belgian flag.

To give an idea of the importance attached to such events, it is sufficient to say that the two small flags that we had brought from Athens will be exhibited at the National Museum of Zakynthos.

In the afternoon we drove to the abandoned area near Kalogerata, which is where the ruins of a Franciscan monastery are located. These brethren had found a dying Vesalius on the neighbouring beach and buried him in the graveyard that has disappeared by now. Despite the rain, a good farmer, the President of the City Council of the hamlet of Pantocrator, was waiting for us, in the company of two constables of the village and some residents. One of them handed me a wreath of wild flowers, which I laid at the foot of the memorial plaque. Then the President took a piece of paper from his pocket on which he had scrawled some verses as simple as they were moving. A well-known folk poet of the city of Kalogerata had climbed up, and with all his heart, and not without emotion, recited a poem in honour of the great Belgian anatomist.

I thanked all of them, with words that praised the beautiful landscape and the particularly cordial atmosphere that I will always remember. Vesalius, I added, could not have found a better environment for his final resting place.

After that, a young shepherd approached me with a dish full of jam and a glass of fresh water which was drawn from the only remnant of the old monastery of the Franciscians.

The ceremony, which took place atop of the mountain full of olive trees and across a huge bay where a similarly raging sea had killed Vesalius, was very moving and was enhanced by the simple and spontaneous expressions of sympathy for Belgium.

Here I put the pastoral report of the then ambassador on hold for a moment. After Nicolas Barbianis, and long before the sailing searchers, the hill had created another victim: that much is obvious. As I said before, the memorial stone has disappeared, stolen, it is assumed. The well is still there today, and exerts an unlikely attraction.

If the story of the search for the grave of Vesalius has been given a new impetus, it is due to the energy which Pascale Pollier and Ann Van de Velde have felt here. If this radiation does not come from Vesalius, it is nevertheless emanating from the Middle Ages and cannot be ignored. After rumours that the memorial stone was perhaps thrown into the well, Pollier has even made plans to lower a camera down into the depths.

A flash-forward: when I visited the site in 2013, in the company of the two archaeologists, they were sure it was old and, indeed, perhaps from the Middle Ages. The masonry is simple and sloppy. The well is protected by a more recently hewn stone ring.

However, what raises questions is that the well is situated atop a hill. A worker from the vicinity confirmed that the water level in the neighbourhood is indeed high, but that the well dries during the summer. Archaeologists are convinced that it is only for the drainage of rainwater and that the well is certainly not a source, as our former ambassador thought.

There are no other signs of human activity around the well apart from agricultural. A few metres from the well, against the wall of a new villa, there is a deep trench and a freshly dug pit. There are no terracotta tiles or other documents here to get excited about. There are some pieces that the archaeologists described as 'halo' or 'background noise', but these probably originate from fertilizer. Where the interviewed witnesses had seen the terracotta roof tiles that Barbianis spoke of, is not clear, but certainly they are not on this side of the hill.

This is undoubtedly an idyllic place, even according to our historians who are accustomed to such views, but 'the site does not offer enough material either historically, geographically or legally to justify entering into the controversy', say our contemporary specialists. This is confirmed by the archaeological service of Zakynthos who has never systematically investigated the site, which also gives a very clear message. The service has checked the launching of the unfortunate constructions on the site, as is customary in this country; that control, however, has not yielded anything either.

Back to December 1960.

> At the end of the afternoon, Mr Barbianis gave a speech on Vesalius in the great hall of the Prefecture. The audience included all the dignitaries and more than three hundred avid listeners, the elite of the island. I was in the audience and heard the speaker thank his audience for their attention. I myself spoke a few words about my historic compatriot, who is rightly called the father of anatomy. It is the memory of Vesalius symbolizing cooperation and friendship that binds our country to Greece.
>
> In the evening the mayor offered a dinner at which, once again, everyone was present, including the Member of Parliament representing the island, Mr Denis Romas and other notables. The Mayor, the President of the Medical Association and Mr Romas each have expressed belief in the close ties with our country. I also had my turn again to thank them and emphasize our love of freedom and the new ties that have been added by their membership in NATO, the alliance that our common ideals of freedom add to the old agreements between the two countries defending democracy.
>
> On the other hand I alluded to the forthcoming entry of Greece into the European Economic Community, which will create an additional bond between us.
>
> I am convinced that these events, which include the island of Zakythos, will certainly have a happy effect on our bilateral relations.

Here endeth the ambassador his report on his pilgrimage to Vesalius in 1960.

In the early sixties Nicolas Barbianis published two more books: *Andreas Vesalius, father of anatomy and the island of Zante,* in 1961, and *The shipwreck and the death of the great anatomist Vesalius,* in 1963.

When, in October 1964, Nicolas Barbianis was invited to Brussels, as a delegate of the island and as Secretary of the Ethnological and Historical Society of Greece, to attend the Fourth Centennial of the death of Andreas Vesalius, he took with him an urn that contained some earth from this very spot on the island.

I had seen a picture of that urn in the journals of Barbianis. In translation, the inscription reads as follows:

> '1564–1964 – In this small amphora is kept the sacred soil that received the remains of the famous Belgian and noble son, the great anatomist Andreas Vesalius, at the place Kalogerata in Laganas Bay on the island of Zakynthos, where, after a shipwreck, he died and was buried.'

I asked myself out loud, and in an e-mail, where that vase was today. Maurice Biesbrouck was curious too and Omer Steeno found it in 2013 in the French-speaking department of the Royal Academy of Medicine in Brussels. In an article about some memorabilia, he shows the urn as it remains there in the same condition as I saw it in the album of Barbianis.

On Zakynthos that fourth centennial was commemorated with a year's delay. On May 1, 1965, on the beach of Laganas, a new memorial was unveiled. The photographs and records of the visitors show that Laganas was still undeveloped and was an open space, with just a few olive trees. It remained unspoiled until about 2000. A few years later, everything was crammed with hotels and restaurants.

At the invitation of Nicolas Barbianis, Secretary General of the Organizing Committee, an impressive delegation of Belgians came to Zakynthos in 1965: Ambassador C. Schuurmans from Athens accompanied by Prof. Dr. Gerard Van der Schueren, Anatomy KU Leuven; Prof. Dr. J. Dankmeijer, Professor of Anatomy and rector at the university of Leiden; Dr. Franz-Andre Sondervorst, Chair of the History of Medicine at UCL and KUL.

On the advice of Omer Steeno I, afterwards, went looking for Dr. C. Spiliopoulos, then President of the Belgian University Alumni in Greece. When I found his successor, he wanted nothing more than to forget that time.

That memorial stone will remain one of our most important landmarks. As the missing tombstone of Kalogerata, however, this stone is also disputed today, but for different reasons, because Belgium has changed so much in the meantime. The monument states in Latin: 'Obituary, tomb of Andreas Vesalius from Brussels who died October 15, 2014, at the age of fifty, upon his return from Jerusalem'.

OBITUARY
ANDREAE VESALII BRUXELLENSIS
TUMULUS
QUI ORBIIT IDIBUS OCTOBRIS ANNO MDLXIV
AETATIS VERO SUAE L
QUUM HIEROSOLYMUS REDISSET

In response to a newsletter from the Embassy of Belgium in which I described the stone, an indignant Flemish compatriot remembers his visit to the memorial as follows. He refers first to the Greek text that precedes the Latin epitaph quoted above:

> "Here died the great Belgian humanist Andre Vesal. This stone was erected in 1965 by the union of Greeks who gained their qualifications in Belgian university institutions."

He continued: 'As a Flemish-speaking Belgian, I was naturally quite disappointed. As a Belgian I simply thought: "C'est ainsi qu'on écrit l' histoire [This is how history is written]…" Belgian humanist? In a period of history where there were no "Belgians"? Vesalius, in his time, probably considered himself an inhabitant of the (then united) Netherlands or as descendant of Brussels, Brabant. His mother tongue was Flemish. There was certainly no talk of "Belgians". His contemporaries Brueghel and Rubens are still universally labelled as Flemish painters. "Andre Vesal" is displayed in French on the monument; would the name Vesalius sound too Flemish, I wonder? Moreover, his original Flemish name is carefully concealed. Concerning the association of Greek students in Belgium, they obviously studied in the French departments of Leuven, Liege and Brussels. They probably didn't encounter that much of the Flemish culture and history. Who can blame them? But was the Embassy of Belgium in Athens in 1965 not competent to provide an appropriate text? The Greeks, who read this record, now get the impression that Belgium is an old nation that brought forth great humanists in the 16th century.'

So there we have the accusation of this pro-Flemish compatriot addressed to his Embassy in Greece.

A day after the unveiling of the monument of the Greek alumni on May 1, 1965, the festivities continued. On that second day, another bust of Vesalius was unveiled on the square behind the library that five years earlier had become the Plateia Andrea Vesal (the Andrea Vesal Square), when Count d'Aspremont-Lynden, and one of my predecessors N. Martacos, Consul of the Embassy of Belgium, came over from Athens.

Today, the square is named after the former mayor, Fotis Ladikos, father of the current Vice-Mayor of Culture, Youth and Sports, Akis Ladikos. Even earlier, before the earthquake, there was a Vesalius Street here, the Odos Vessaliou, with a double s. Another Vesalius Square (Plateia Andrea Vesalionos) previously lay in the open space in front of Santa Maria delle Grazie, which was then still located at the sea shore.

Since the sixties, no more new monuments have been erected in honour of Vesalius. In 2012 a series of articles of Dionyssios Serras and Ioannis Demetis appeared in the local press. The latter in particular

Illust. 8:
On the beach of Laganas, May 1, 1965

←
Illus. 9:
On the Andrea Vesal Square, Zakynthos, May 2, 1965.

praised the efforts of Nicolas Barbianis in keeping the memory of Vesalius alive. In this article the audience is reminded that the bust has been moved to the middle of the square, to be more visual.

Nicolas Barbianis is modestly present in the Museum of Solomos and Kalvos in Zakynthos. I regularly stand in front of his bronze bust on the wooden column, just above the stairs to the first floor. Just around the corner, the coat of arms of the family Barbianis decorates the wall between those of the noble families of the island. It already became clear from the book of Nicolas Barbianis that one of his ancestors, Dionysios Barbianis (1788–1866) was a well-known writer of the island and an initiated freedom fighter, and as such also present in the museum.

In the margin of a deed of land in Kalogerata in 1741, it is also said that ten years later the Venetian Count Ricardo Barbianis was the first statesman of Zakynthos. And Omer Steeno discovered a publication from which he presumes 'that Nicolas Barbianis and his grandson Nikos Varvianis are descendants of Count Barbiano the Belgiojoso, Minister Plenipotentiary to Belgium from 1783 to 1787!' Was he perhaps the son of the first leader of Zakynthos, who was sent to Belgium as an Ambassador? That would not surprise me. Nikos, born in 1960 as son of Menelaos Moschonas and Liza Varvianis, daughter of Nicolas, still has links with Belgian nobility. When I met his mother, she emotionally spoke French.

With the death of Barbianis on June 28, 1980, it became somewhat quieter around Andreas Vesalius on Zakynthos in Greece. Nikos Varvianis maintains the legacy of his grandfather. For many years, he has left the office of Nicolas Barbianis untouched. Only recently, he had to give in to the pressure of the current occupant of the property to expand the pharmacy. In doing this the office and study of Barbianis has disappeared. The furniture, archives and lithography of Milster, after the painting of Edouard Hamman from Ostend, were saved and moved.

At the invitation of Nikos Varvianis, I had the chance to visit the family estate among the olive groves in Romiri more than once. I was particularly impressed by the Panagia Vlahema Chapel, next to the house. It was in this chapel that grandfather Nicolas hid the manuscripts of Dionysios Solomos and the archives of the Star of the East from the Nazis during the war. Nicolas Barbianis stayed in this area from 1930 to 1980. As was common in many similar churches on the island, this chapel was also used almost daily by the family, and for social occasions. Since 2007, that is no longer allowed by the Greek Orthodox Church.

Nikos Varvianis and his family settled here from the nineties. Since then, and especially after a severe storm in 2003, he has worked steadily on the renovation of the chapel. In 2011, the chapel underwent a professional refurbishing, in the framework of the international 'Romiri Project'. This collaboration between the International Centre for the Study of the Preservation and Restoration of Cultural Property (ICCROM), the University of York and the Greek Ministry of Culture has been extensively documented. I made these notes from the accompanying booklet.

The magnificent ceiling paintings on wood are Italian, so that you do not feel like you're in the Zakynthian countryside. But you will be immediately reminded of that when you stand on the hill, barely ten metres on the other side of the house. The view is magnificent from the plateau adorned by a historic column and a plaque in which

Nicolas Barbianis had carved a verse of the 'Sonnet to Zante' (1837) by Edgar Allan Poe. Although he wrote it to the memory of a lost love, Barbianis saw the lines as a reference to the earthquakes that so often destroy the fertile island.

On a sweltering summer's day, I ran through all the rows of the Central Cemetery of Zakynthos, again and again, searching for the grave of Nicolas Barbianis. A day later, after I had called in the help of Pavlos Plessas, I stood before a simple little plot against the outside wall, not far from the entrance gate, opposite the grave of a colleague consul where I had earlier spent too much time in perusal. On the high classical column is this inscription:

all family members of
N. Barbianis
May 26, 1879
resting under this tombstone
hope
that their dust
will unite with his

10. The anatomist and the biomedical artist

Fate, give me no foreign grave
Death is only sweet
When we sleep
in our own home land

the most frequently quoted verse of
'The Patriot' in 'Odes'
by Andreas Kalvos,
born in 1792 in Zakynthos,
translated by Richard Stoneman (1994).

With, I can imagine, a profound homesickness, Andreas Ioannidis Kalvos was writing these verses in a grey and rainy England, where he was languishing, if not fading away, as a poor teacher. No one knows what Andreas Kalvos looked like. There is no known portrait of him. All we know is that he indulged in walking around in the English countryside 'completely dressed in black', according to Konstantinos Demaras in his account on Modern Greek literature.

Pascale Pollier is interested in making a facial reconstruction of his skull, but would his tomb in the Solomos and Kalvos museum ever be allowed to be opened? How he arrived there, on this Greek St Mark's Square, brought in from a forgotten grave in the English countryside, is a story to be told here for more than one reason.

Fate did not listen to his pleas to die peacefully at home. From 1869, when he drew his last breath, until 1960, ninety-one years later, he had been lying, certainly without any peace, next to his second English wife in a cemetery in Keddington.

Then the Greek poet and Nobel laureate George Seferis succeeded in putting the bones of Kalvos and his wife on Olympic Airways flight 410, on Saturday, March 19, 1960, to be flown to Athens. Upon their scheduled arrival, they were met by the elite of the country, though the people of Greece didn't see anything of it: the newspapers were on strike that day.

George Seferis was Ambassador of Greece in London at that time; he had previously served there as a Consul. Much earlier, in 1941/42, he had saved Kalvos from oblivion by republishing his poems. 'As a poet, he died in his 34th year,' Seferis wrote, but, I would add, as a man he died at seventy-eight.

He might have been resuscitated as a poet, but his grave had still not been recovered at that time. The story of that quest sounds familiar: listed in records, visited by travellers, forgotten because of the outbreak of war, once again neglected and overgrown, bureaucracy and red tape, strikes. In short: it was not until 1960 when the poet of homesickness returned home.

The efforts of Seferis show that he considered this task to have been one of his more important duties. I also understand the thought process of Nicolas Barbianis better now, as he wondered whether the newly independent Belgium was looking for Andreas Vesalius because they may have been planning to repatriate his bones. When it became clear that none of my predecessors ever had that intention, Barbianis himself brought that urn with 'sacred earth that had received his remains' to the home country of the anatomist.

As a taphophile with a diplomatic passport, I never considered this as my job. Quite the contrary. An anecdote that I'll relate with some embarrassment makes perfectly clear how I, and my employers, think about compatriots who stayed behind in foreign lands.

The absolutely first report that I ever signed myself, in the absence of the Head of Mission, and sent to the home administration, was the announcement that I had discovered the neglected grave of a Belgian consul on the Tanzanian island of Zanzibar. He had died of dysentery, sometime in the early 1830s. My question, whether a modest budget could be made available to restore the grave with a lick of paint and a new metal chain, has remained unanswered since 1990.

From Zanzibar to Zakynthos I hardly changed my view. Just leave them between the spices there and the flowers here. We'll find them anyway and worship them on the spot.

That must be exactly what Pascale Pollier and Ann Van de Velde thought when, one day in the spring, they left, for the first time, for the island the Venetians called the Flower of the Levant, to find the grave of Vesalius, probably from a drizzly Belgium. With some sense of the symbolism, they did so with sailing doctors from the Medical Yacht Club of Belgium.

On Tuesday May 25 2010, they met then vice-mayor of Zakynthos and orthopedic surgeon Dr. D. Aktipis. The pair also visited Katerina Demeti in the Museum of Solomos.

Earlier they had gone, by taxi, to take a look at where their idol had perhaps washed up in Laganas. At their question about where he could have been buried, the taxi driver took them to a graveyard where only recent graves were to be seen, 'on top of much older tombs,' he clarified. The willing man also phoned a priest. This is the latter's resume: 'The people of Zakynthos were frightened of Vesalius because he cut people open. He was a magician and not allowed to be buried with Zakynthians. He was taken to a secret place, away from the people.' End of quote, from a conversation with an unknown priest.

A day later they had several conversations in the hospital of Zakynthos, especially with Pavlos Kapsambelis, a surgeon and President of the Medical Association of Zakynthos and the Ionian Islands, who seemed very preoccupied with the history of the Belgian anatomist on the island. He called on the assistance of fellow physicians, one of whom supposedly had published a study on Vesalius. The two of them even brought Pollier and Van de Velde to Kalogerata, which is where many suspect the tomb of Vesalius to be.

On the idyllic hillside overlooking the bay of Laganas, Pollier and Van de Velde discovered that a huge construction was being built there. Judging by the enormous concrete slab they saw, just past the turn to the hamlet of Pantokratoras, they assumed that it would become a hotel. A bit further from the main road, between the olive and cypress trees, they saw that a spacious villa, with impressive walls, was being erected.

Their guide from the hospital told them that, a few years ago, he had been there, looking for the commemoration stone that Nicolas Barbianis had established. He had shot a roll of more than fifty photos of this site. The doctor remembered that the stone had been damaged or broken, probably during the earthquake of August 12, 1953, but that it still stood upright. Unfortunately, he added, in 2010 he had lost the photos and the negatives. Of the stone that indicated the place where Andreas Vesalius had supposedly died, between the walls of a vanished monastery, no trace was left.

The two doctors had a very heated discussion with the owner and his father, who claimed that they had never seen a memorial here. Even more to the point, they added that there had never been a monastery or a Franciscan chapel nearby. 'Even though we could see "that" with our own eyes,' Pollier wrote to me, referring to an old well, just before the entrance to the villa.

The group was evicted from the private property. They secretly took some pictures that they later compared to old reports of the memorial. On the basis of favourable comparisons with the surrounding landscape, they are sure that they had been standing at exactly the right place. They had included in their calculations the coordinates of the location with a GPS. 'We were really standing on the grave of the great anatomist Andreas Vesalius,' Pascale Pollier wrote with excitement.

Back at the Hospital of Zakynthos they told their story to Pavlos Kapsambelis who promised that he would make the news of the neglect of the tomb of Vesalius, public at a press conference. Our compatriots assured him that they would warn the respective embassies in Belgium and Athens. All would do anything to avoid 500 years of history being lost without a trace.

Quite soon after the trip, the former Director of the Belgian School, Steven Soetens, worded their dismay to the very competent archaeological service in Zakynthos. The fact that he took this step was to his credit, but everyone involved was conscious that the information provided was mainly hearsay.

His email of 21 June 2010 created quite a stir on the island, and to this day this incident is not yet completely forgotten. He repeats the elements Pascale Pollier has brought together.

He was worried, he writes, that the remains of Andreas Vesalius were threatened, and what's more, that the monument that had been unveiled by the Belgian Ambassador in 1965 had disappeared.

This date is obviously a mistake, and it's not the first time that the monument (which was placed on the beach, and inaugurated in 1965 by the Ambassador) is confused with the stone of Barbianis of 1952, which was visited by the envoy in 1960. Later Omer Steeno would remind Pascale Pollier of a similar mistake.

Steven Soetens then developed in his mail the two hypotheses about the exact location of the grave. There is, indeed, the Santa Maria, in the same place where the tomb of Cicero had been discovered, twenty years before the death of Vesalius. And there is the second, more plausible theory, according to the director of the EBSA, pointing to the hamlet of Kalogerata. Here Soetens refers undoubtedly to George Sarton, a source that was provided by Pollier. Indeed, it has been said that Vesalius died 'in loco et deserto in miserrimo tuguriolo' (on a deserted beach in a poor hut), probably where once stood the convent of the lost Aghii Theodorii, the Holy Theodoors.

All this is scientifically difficult to ascertain, but lives on as a story in the heads of many, he would comment later. The following sentences in particular draw the brow in a frown. I quote: 'I think there is little archaeological evidence, but the importance of Vesalius is so great that we cannot take any risk and should make every effort to ensure that an archaeologist will follow up the works at this site.' With this he suggests that it should not be too great an effort to exercise some kind of control.

'I've also heard that the owner of the land is working as a secretary for the current Mayor of Laganas, and that he allows no one on that spot. If his interests are mainly economic (and probably they are), then I can understand that. Yet he should remember that his land is worth even more if it turns out that Vesalius is indeed buried there. And even if that would not be so, then the disappearance of the monument would be unacceptable and immediate action must be taken. Reportedly Gert Jan van Wijngaarden, Dutch archaeologist on Zakynthos, saw the monument until 2009. Today that statue has disappeared.'

That's as far as the letter goes.

The answers of the Mayor of Laganas and the archaeological service came in quite fast. Mayor Dionysios Komiotis said that he did not know of a monument in Kalogerata and that no secretary in his service lives there.

'This is an empty accusation and is wrong information,' he responded. There is, of course, still the monument on the beach of Laganas that, incidentally is called Vesal, where annually a swimming contest, called Vesalia, is organized. He goes on to say that he will ensure that this monument is restored to its original state.

The head of the local archaeological service, Diamando Rigakou, answered that the service visited Kalogerata and no monument was found. The mayor informed the archaeological service that during his entire term of office no monument had been seen there. It must therefore have been removed before 2009. He is in agreement with those who believe that the monument must have disappeared during the great earthquake of 1953.

I later received this comprehensive report from Constantinos (Kostas) Geladas, the President of the Council of Pantocratores: 'The said monument was destroyed after 1996 (as indicated on the back of the coloured picture of the inscription of the monument), but it is also said that is still stood there in 2004.'

Nobody knows when exactly the monument disappeared. Out of ordinary neglect? Is there a political dimension to the case? Are personal scores settled by the affair? Is the intention, politically or personally, to repudiate the work of Nicolas Barbianis?

His hypothesis may be obsolete, but it is no less valuable. Feelings are obviously running high because the monument is indeed a symbol of one of the longest running theories about the grave of Vesalius. The fact that an ancient monument has disappeared remains annoying. There is a complaint filed. The police and the courts have been investigating and have been questioning. It is not clear when the outcome will be made public.

11. The anatomist and his unwept grave

Tu non altro che il canto avrai del figlio,
o materna mia terra;
a noi prescrisse il fato illacrimata sepoltura.

Of your son Vesalius will only remain this song,
O mother's land! My doom
Is exile and an unwept sepulchre.

paraphrasing 'Sonnet VI' by Ugo Foscolo, (Greek) Italian poet,
born in 1778 in Zakynthos,
from *Sepulchres,* a collection of translater J.G. Nichols, 2009.

The romantic poets Andreas Kalvos and Ugo Foscolo have at least one thing in common: both were born in Zakynthos, Kalvos in 1792 and Foscolo in 1778. They met in Italy in 1813 and Kalvos very soon became secretary to the already famous Foscolo. In late 1816, they travelled together to Great Britain, but a few months later they fell out and each went his own way. Kalvos left for a life full of romance, revolution and travel, voyaging from Italy, where he was involved with the secret Movement of the Carbonari, over Switzerland and France to Corfu.

Foscolo, otherwise known as Nikolaos Phoskolos, stayed behind in England, poor and lonely. He was barely 49 when, in 1827, he was buried in Chiswick on the Thames in London. In 1852, Kalvos returned to England and lived to an old age: he died in 1869. Luckily for him, he did not have to live through the experience of watching the remains of his compatriot, friend and employer, Ugo Foscolo, be exhumed from the moist soil of England in 1871 and brought with Italian state ceremony to Florence where he now rests in the company of Galileo and Machiavelli in the Gothic Fransciscan Church of the Cross.

That Kalvos had to wait for almost one hundred years to have a similar but Greek state ceremony is an irony of history which amuses me greatly. He now rests next to the official poet laureate Dionysios Solomos in the mausoleum museum in Zakynthos.

Central to my taphophile library is also the book *Last Letters of Jacopo Ortis* by Ugo Foscolo, and a special bonus: 'Of Tombs, an ode for Ippolito Pindemonte'. This is a pamphlet in verse railing against the regulation imposed by Napoleon in Italy, which ruled that cemeteries should be positioned outside of the centre of the city and that tombstones must be kept simple and identical.

> '*Deorum manium iura sancta sunto*, indicates classical Roman law:
> do not interfere with the rights of holy shadows.'

Another collection of Foscolo's poetry is *Sepulchres*, selected and translated by J.G. Nichols, with the sonnets and the verse that opens this chapter. Foscolo writes about Homer and his song, Odysseus, but I can only see before me the lost Vesalius and his *Fabrica* in these verses. These are men of my heart, these grave-romancers Kalvos and Foscolo, who believe that the shadows of the dead are inviolable.

From 16 to 23 December 2011, having arranged an appointment with Pascale Pollier and co on Zakynthos, I took the opportunity to search for traces of Kalvos and Foscolo. I succeeded in finding a mausoleum for one and a theatre for the other around the corner; an ordinary bust for one, for the other a commorative stone with a mourning angel on the location where his house once stood in the street that carries his name. Later on I would meet Nikias Lountzis, who is fascinated by the history of the island, to the extent that he is driven to rebuild the house of Foscolo. Of Andreas Vesalius I only discovered the portrait bust and one of two commorative stones.

Pascale Pollier, Ann Van de Velde and Marc De Roeck had flown to Zakynthos for the second time. I arrived by car having experienced a day's delay from Athens. On the ferry we met just a few or no tourists, but a lot of popes, priests and imposing bishops.

We hoped to witness the procession of the patron saint of the island, St Dionysios. Together with the priests, we were eager to see his relics paraded around town, as happens twice a year: in August to celebrate the arrival of his remains on Zakynthos, and in December to commemorate his death almost one hundred years before.

When we drove at dusk from the harbour alongside the Dionysios Church, we heard from inside the litanies of the choir and were still hopeful. But the Zakynthians had already carried around the mummy of their patron saint and had set off all their fireworks at once during the day. We would not be able to experience the nocturnal procession with torches, fireworks, singing and dancing, during which the orthodox saint usually would appear to approve of the god of the same name awakening the earth every year and helping us to forget the dark winter. Due to December rains we missed this procession.

The day before my arrival, the trio had driven back to Laganas/Vesal and Kalogerata full of expectations. The neighbourhood where Nicolas Barbianis suspects Vesalius's grave to be, continued to have an insatiable attraction for them. With a rental car, they explored and filmed the whole neighbourhood, in particular the stalled construction, which continued to intrigue them. What was subsequently described as a possible project for a hotel or a horse riding school turned out to be a diving centre. They had heard that a Dutch diving instructor once worked for the owner and that would be their excuse if they were to bump into him. That indeed occurred, but they didn't learn anything from the encounter.

It so happened that they were staying in a guesthouse which was managed by a retired topographer. The art-loving man showed some old maps and drawings of the old coastline from his library. Upon his suggestion, we set off together from the white Vesalius bust on what was once the Vesalius Square and is now called Ladikos square. The friendly keeper of a newspaper kiosk once proudly showed me her electricity bill, still addressed to the Vesalius Square.

From there, we walked on foot to the other side of the city. Van Wijngaarden had informed our Vesalius searching compatriots about a tennis court opposite a hotel on the coastline that some consider to possibly cover the burial place of Vesalius. Not only did we photograph that particular tennis court from all corners, but also every little church and park in the area.

I received a similar indication from Els De Lobel, Honorary Consul of Belgium on Corfu, who had heard once from compatriots that he was probably buried under a park or square opposte a hotel on the coast.

Later I concluded that these compatriots probably were better informed than us: might this particular hotel perhaps be the Palatino Hotel? And the square they were referring to the somewhat wide crossing of Kolokotroni and Kolyva Streets where we today situate the Santa Maria delle Grazie?

For the rest of this trip we were all surfing on emotion and hearsay. I'm writing this down rather hesitantly, but what were we actually hoping to find? That the missing church with the tomb of Vesalius would appear out of nowhere, as in the old days a landscape would emerge from the negative onto photographic paper in a bath of chemicals? That the fata morgana would appear, not in reality, but in pixels on the screen? Were we expecting a miracle?

The sad truth is that we then walked from the wrong park to the wrong church. Nervously we walked around the 16th century chapel, which is on the original coastline. At the gate, under the clock, is written the year of its construction: 1511.

Faintly visible in the choir, on looking through a crack in the wall, we could see carved wooden panels that we desperately tried to photograph.

Pavlos Plessas thinks it is in the vicinity of this Estavromenos Church (or the Church of the Crucified Christ) that Vesalius's ship dropped its anchor and that this is where he collapsed.

In the first half of the 17th century the gates of the city were situated there. Just above the Estavromenos Church, on the hill, is the Church of Santa Veneranda, known as Agia Paraskevi, and just around the corner of this church is a spring; the fountain that is there, probably dating from 1203, was renovated in 1760. A little further into the bay is the well-known well of Kryoneri.

Van de Velde and De Roeck returned to Belgium; Pollier and I completed a few official visits. To be succesful this search for the lost grave of Vesalius indeed had to be made official.

One of the first appointments was the rather uncomfortable meeting with the archaeologist of the Byzantine Museum, who reminded us immediately of the accusing letter and its reponse. Also our visit of the hospital, Pollier will remember. We indeed had some meetings at the old hospital, then still in the city centre. We were thrown back and forth between doctors who seemed inexplicably nervous. Telephones went off and on until Pavlos Kapsambelis, President of the Medical Society, appeared. Pollier had already met him during her first visit. We were dealing with a Friend of Vesalius, that much was obvious. In some offices we discovered prints from the *Fabrica*. Of our conversations with Kapsambelis a lot was lost in translation.

On our way to another appointment, we were addressed in perfect English by a man we didn't know. Assertively he recalled the story of the stolen commemorative stone: did we realize what kind of a hornets' nest we had ventured into? Did we know about the intrigue that surrounded this subject? The questions sounded innocent, but seemed to carry a threat not to interfere any further. We never learned who this man was and the whole conversation was quite menacing. Especially our artist wasn't very at ease in the following days.

This first official visit was widely covered in the local press. On December 20, 2011, the local newspaper *Ermis*, announced the commemorations in 2014 on its front page. In the paper, more information was given about the visit of the 'Belgian Consul' to 'Mayor Stelios Bozikis'. The *Imera* newspaper shows several pictures. The copy of the antique map of Zakynthos that I received on this occasion still hangs in my study. The local television broadcast a report of the visit that evening. Many of the photos and articles from the press coverage have been included in the Vesalius brochure, a publication of the Embassy of Belgium in which I announced the Vesalius commemorations.

12. Vesalius Momentum I: Athens

A phenomenon oiled by blood,
Made of unequal parts like a Cellini.
Saltcellar.
A little gold and a little charcoal.
A little bone, a little wax.
A little alcohol, a little horror and a little gum.
A little ivory,
A little sulphur,
A little damp dust,
A sluice of fluids.
Twenty-four pulleys,
one hundred counterweights, two lenses, dark shadows, swivels, a syringe, chords,
strings, sins, shit, teeth, nails
and various random involuntary motions.

'Vesalius Song' of Louis Andriessen,
in the film *M is Man, Music, Mozart*, directed by Peter Greenaway, 1991.

Under the umbrella of 'Things of Belgium', the Ambassador of Belgium in Athens, Marc Van den Reeck, developed a concept in which Belgian companies sponsoring cultural events organized by the Embassy are offered a platform to extend their commercial, political and diplomatic network. Since 2011, we have organized more than thirty concerts in Athens and the rest of Greece. From the beginning we tried to widen the musical scope that we could offer. The first lecture, which we called 'Vesalius Momentum', has since been followed by several editions in Greece and in Belgium.

The catalyst was a long-expected trip to Greece by Omer Steeno, who on his way to Easter in Corfu, stayed in Athens for 24 hours. I invited him along with his entire group of a Flemish cultural travel agency. Pollier, Van de Velde and none other than Mark Richard Gardiner joined us in Athens to mark this first momentum.

We also created this event to present the Vesalius brochure that I had written that spring to announce the festivities for 2014. Written in a few days only, it still has some allure thanks to the expensive edition on glossy paper sponsored by the Honorary Consul of Belgium in Thessaloniki, Alexander Bakatselos.

The event took place on April 10, 2012, at the Dutch Institute of Athens. The Director was our compatriot Christiane Tytgat, who after her assignment as the Director of the Belgian School stayed on in Greece.

Illustrated with sixteenth-century harpsichord music performed by Jerassimos Coidan, a Greek musician trained in Belgium, a projection of online prints of the *Fabrica*, and fragments of the 'Vesalius Song' from Peter Greenaway's film, the celebrations of 2014 were presented.

Steeno formulated a preliminary answer to the question, *Who* is Vesalius? Gardiner (President of the Vesalius Steering Committee of the UK) presented the congress by answering the question *what*? Pollier and Van de Velde spoke about how far they had travelled in the search for the remains of the anatomist. *Where*, they wondered. I tried to find an answer to the question of *why* Vesalius inspired me and others. Why indeed? Perhaps when in a melancholic mood, the text may offer some clues as to why the taphophile in me refuses to die.

'In the Acknowledgements of our booklet, Andreas Vesalius confesses that he's contagious, infecting everybody who touches him with a virus.

In 2005, in a poll searching for The Greatest Belgian, Andreas Vesalius was chosen 6th in Flanders and 19th in Wallonia. What could be the explanation of such an epidemic? How does a medieval scientist end up in the company of Eddy Merckx and Jacques Brel? Why is Vesalius an inspiration for so many artists and scientists, of yesterday and today?

For many, Vesalius, the man, is synonymous with the images of his dissected cadavers as shown in his seven books about the structure of the human body: the *Humani Corporis Fabrica Libri Septem*, published for the first time in 1543 (when he was only 28).

Professor Steeno showed me his duplicate of the *Fabrica*. Just touching and going through this heavyweight book is a physical and emotional experience. The dense texts and studies of the human body are overwhelming: musclemen, skeletons, organs and bones.

Scientists view this differently, but we, common mortals, are simultaneously disgusted and attracted by his work. What we see are not merely human beings but an expression of their mortality. Vesalius's dissected humans move casually in landscapes and interiors and we thus easily recognize our own decay. What we see is our destiny.

"Madame, all stories, if continued far enough, end in death, and he is no true-story teller who would keep that from you." Ernest Hemingway.

Like every good story, Vesalius's history is one of death. And that's a first explanation of his success.

In 1991 the British film director Peter Greenaway made *M is for Man, Music and Mozart*, a visual and acoustic cocktail of animation, theatre and dance. A woman sings a chain of words, alphabetically. Reaching M, the 13th and central letter of the alphabet, the gods decide to create man. Now that man can move, he needs Music, and according to Peter Greenaway, Mozart is the perfect music.

Although the movie is set in a medieval dissection theatre, Peter Greenaway doesn't reflect on Vesalius as a metaphor for death but as a metaphor for life. Based upon a dissection inspired by Vesalius, a new man is constructed. Death and life are the head and tail of a flipped coin.

I'll complete my equation: like every good story, Vesalius's history is one of death and of life, as in 'the meaning of life', for Peter Greenaway translated in Music and Mozart; figuratively speaking, in Arts and Science'.

In 1969 the British composer Sir Peter Maxwell Davies also confronts a facsimile of *The humani corporis fabrica*. He selects fourteen anatomical studies and re-creates them as the fourteen Stations of the Cross. His theatre work for dancer, solo cello and instrumental ensemble, *Vesalii Icones*, becomes a Via Dolorosa.

As does Greenaway, Maxwell Davis serves a cocktail of medieval religious music and early twentieth century popular music, shaken but not stirred with his own idiom. Dance movements are inspired by poses sketched by Vesalius. The anatomist has become a choreographer, directing a contemporary Jesus Christ. Vesalius's studies have become religious icons.
The climax of this ballet is of course the resurrection, but to our surprise or even shock, it is not Christ but a medieval antichrist who emerges from the grave. "Some may consider such an interpretation sacrilegious," Davis has written, "but the point

I am trying to make is a moral one. It is a matter of distinguishing the false from the real, that one should not be taken in by appearances."

Religious or sacrilegious, Davis has seen the spiritual dimension we all imagine in Vesalius's history.

I'll complete my equation a third time: Vesalius's history is attractive because his story offers, through Arts and Science, an answer to our fears about the finiteness of life.

The performance was an avant-première of the events for 2014 with the central theme: Vesalius, Art and Science. These lectures were followed by a reception.

Due to a strike of the ferries, the distinguished guests from Zakynthos, the mayor, the director of the Solomos Museum and the President of the Medical Association of the island, did not reach Athens. Present were Nikos Varvianis, Greek personalities from the museum, academic and diplomatic world, and Belgian-Greek pharmaceutical and medical companies. Twenty-five companions of Omer Steeno and the committees of the Belgian associations were invited. To my great disappointment, there was little reaction from the 20-or-so invited journalists. How to sell a medieval anatomist I had not yet understood at that point.

CODA

During the Momentum in the Dutch Institute of Athens, I discovered in a magazine stand, the May 2011 issue of the house journal, an article entitled 'Who will be the first to crawl through the window of the ruins of Zakynthos?'

It is the travelogue of poet Mark Boog and photographer Eddo Hartmann, who 'drove around Zakynthos for a week in a red car, to make an artistic portrait of the dilapidated villas, churches, fortresses, bridges and farms. Only the Greek goats did not want to cooperate,' concludes Anne Versloot in her introduction, and she completes the entire article with, among other things: 'They also visited the tourist resort of Zakynthos, Laganas (famous for its many slurred British youth). Not their most favourite place, but still nice to have seen.' Even though the treasure hunting travellers must have passed the Vesalius Monument on the beach, to my disappointment, not one single word is spent on the Brabant anatomist.

The result of their journey (with highlights which include not only 'who first crawls through the window', but also 'climbing over the fence of course') is the glossy book: Zakynthos where eternity lasts sixty years only, a literary and photographic impression of the ruins in Zakynthos.'

On Wednesday, May 23, 2012 the booklet was presented in the National Museum of Antiquities in Leiden. The promising programme stated, among other topics: 'The Zakynthos Archaeology Project, Earthquakes and the Archaeological Landscape of Zakynthos', by Dr Gert Jan van Wijngaarden, and 'Behind the door of Dionysios Tyrogalas, the rediscovery of ancient tombstones from the collection – Roma'.

I quote further of the announcement: 'Every summer, groups of students from Amsterdam travel to Zakynthos to search for shards, flint and a temple. As they walk across the island, they encounter a lot that has nothing to do with archeology: dogs, goats and chickens, local residents, abandoned wells, a single monastery. But they certainly see many ruins: the silent witness of many earthquakes. Meanwhile, the ruins have become the distinctive, eye-catching elements of the Ionian island. Unfortunately, the ruins are increasingly being demolished. Sometimes this is done for security reasons, but mostly because the past stands in the way of developers.'

I inform the home front of the Dutch Zakynthos Day: Pascale Pollier from London and I from Athens cannot make it, but Omer Steeno, Ann Van de Velde and Marc De Roeck immediately register.

The reaction of Professor Steeno is as critical as it is short: 'meant only to raise funds, learned nothing. Despite the high expectations not a single mention of Vesalius.' Marc De Roeck has yet learned something for our quest 'from the presentation on the 84-year-old Dionysios Tyrogalas, who as a contractor and builder has collected a lot of treasures after the devastation in 1953.'

That sentence intrigued me for a while. Is he suggesting that Mr Tyrogalas, who was mainly a shipowner, had something to do with Vesalius? That the remains of his grave or the church are in his possession? That the commemorative stone is kept in his private museum? From his talks with van Wijngaarden, I copy just a few excerpts from the email report: 'When we told him we were Belgians, he immediately understood why we were there. He thought our project to be very interesting and possibly wishes to be involved … but he doesn't believe we will find the bones.'

13. The anatomist and the Zakynthian blogger

In this fragrant isle
Your bones covered by its soil
Your face reflected on marble
Superior is the Grace of thy Glory.

X.K. Goutsis,
'To Andreas Vesalius', in the newspaper *Melon,*
29 April 1965, Zakynthos.

In Greece, the first grave is rarely the final resting place. It happens all the time that a common mortal must pass through a bone gallery or ossuary, before he can return to the earth:

'for out of it wast thou taken
for dust thou art, and unto dust shalt thou return',
so sayeth Genesis, 3:19

Some are even more dragged around than others. Some get home quite soon, others with a century of delay. Still others have not succeeded (yet) or they were just passing through Zakynthos. The thought that the tomb of Vesalius on Zakynthos is his first, makes me hopeful and peaceful simultaneously. A man with such an aura will eventually find the tomb that suits him. He died barely four hundred and fifty years ago; in local, Zakynthian time, that is only seven and a half times eternity. And he is not the only one. If I were to make a list it would appear as follows: Ugo Foscolos, born in Zakynthos and died in London, was primarily an Italian poet; almost half a century passed before he was transferred to exquisite companionship in Florence. The national poet of Greece, Dionysios Solomos, born in Zakynthos, died in Corfu but seven years after his death, in 1865, he was shipped to his hometown in a new coffin. Andreas Kalvos, born in Zakynthos and runner-up for the title of Poet Laureate, had to wait almost a hundred years in the moist soil of England before he could join Solomos. After I saw the movie about Ioannis Varvakis in the Fosolos Cinema, I tried to find the remains of the pirate who died on Zakynthos in 1825, but I was unsuccesful because his bones too were moved around a great deal: from the sanatorium, Lazareto, Pest House in Argasi, to the churchyard of St Catherine on the river and eventually, in 1930 to the First Cemetery in Athens. There one should be able to find also writer Gregorios Xenopoulos who spent his childhood on Zakynthos. I haven't found them yet.

A contemporary of Vesalius, who after his death was awarded very little rest, was the holy Dionysios of Zakynthos. He is literally a walking dead. His mummy is carried around twice a year in a procession. Many believe that he still gets up from his grave to perform miracles. Even his slippers are wearing out, is said here. They are regularly changed. One is exhibited in the Nissos Ferry of Kefalonian Lines. In Greece more walking saints are appearing; the tradition is well known.

This is the story of the death of Dionysius after a life that began in Zakynthos in 1547, when Andreas Vesalius was thirty-three…

When Vesalius was buried, the holy Dionysios was about seventeen years old. According to Pavlos Plessas he lived very close to the Maria delle Grazie Church at the beginning of Kolokotroni Street. Who knows, he might even have witnessed the funeral of our anatomist. He himself died on December 17, 1622. He was buried at Strophades, one of the two tiny islands south of Zakynthos. When, according to local customs, he was exhumed a few years later, he was found to be intact. This has been known to happen from time to time; for example, Saint Gerasimus on Kefalonia and Saint Spiridon on Corfu are both very well preserved too.

As a mummy, the holy Dionysios moved to Crete. Then, fleeing the Turkish-Venetian battle for Crete from 1645–1669, his bones returned to Strophades, from one church to another. In 1716, when the Venetians suppressed the Turkish assault of Zakynthos, the latter turned against the island of Strofades. The monks hid their mummy in a cave, but eventually had to leave him. Like those of Cicero much earlier, his hands were also removed, stolen, sold, and the left one can now be seen on the island of Andros. Even that should not come as a surprise. On Kefalonia, under the pretext of Andreas and Anatomy, I went to greet the right foot of the Apostle Andreas. After the looting, the mummy was brought to Zakynthos on August 22, 1717.

On the anniversary of his arrival in August, Dionyisios is carried in a procession. In December the procession is organized to commemorate his death. It is said that this tradition dates back to 1901, when Archbishop Dionysios Plessas was archbishop of Zakynthos, but I think I have seen illustrations that would date it to an earlier period.

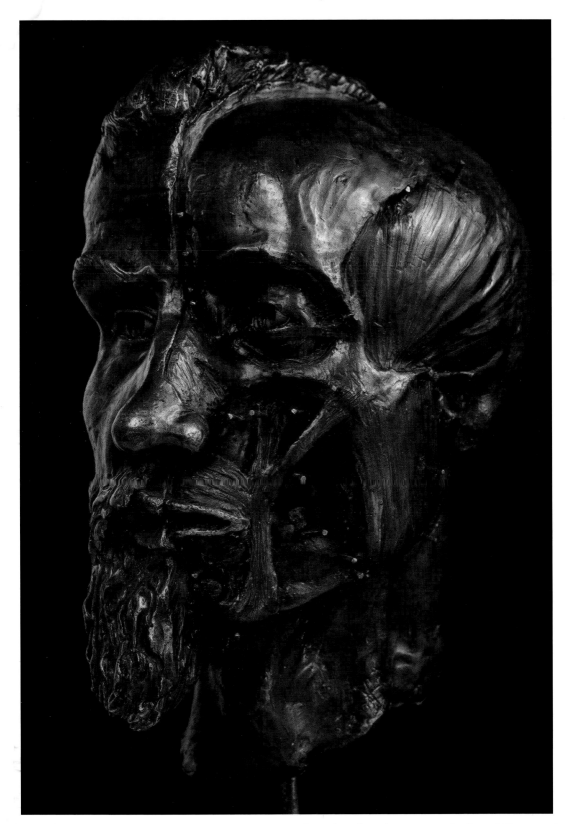

Illus. 1: Facial reconstruction of Vesalius by Richard Neave and Pascale Pollier, photo courtesy St. George's University/ Joshua Yetman, Grenada.

Illus. 2: Franciscan Stone, photo courtesy Maria Sidirokastriti, Zakynthos.

Illus. 3: Coat of arms of Vesalius, sculpted by Chantal Pollier in Belgian marble.

Illus. 4: Plinth of the new Vesalius monument in Zakynthos, sculpted by Chantal Pollier in Zakynthian stone.

Illus. 5: Old well in Kalogerata, Laganas, photo courtesy Chantal Pollier

Legend

Papadatos' map

Modern cadastral map

30 15 0   30 m

N

Illus. 6: Figure 1, Geographical Information System, by Sylviane Déderix, for Laboratory of Geophysical-Satellite Remote Sensing & Archaeo-environment (IMS-FORTH), Crete, Greece.

Legend

Santa Maria delle Grazie

Map of 1892

Papadatos' map

Illus. 7: Figure 2, GIS, idem.

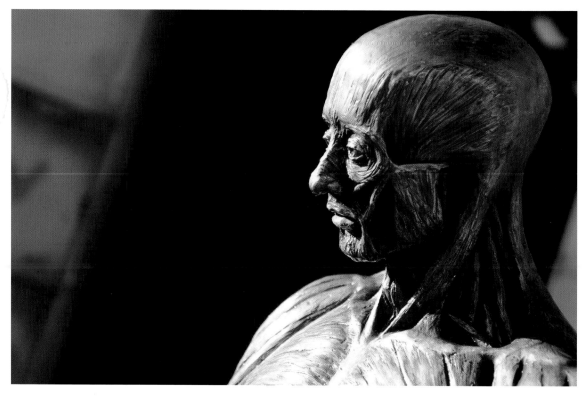

Illus. 8: Detail of the new Vesalius monument in Zakynthos, created by Richard Neave and Pascale Pollier; photo courtesy Jimmy De Clercq, Kunstgieterij/Fonderie De Clercq Ginsberg, Ghent, Belgium.

In our adventure of the quest for the lost tomb of Andreas Vesalius, here too a Plessas plays a role. But we did not realize this at the beginning. A Greek employee of the London designers of our website tipped us off that 'there is a blog from a Greek with family ties in Zakynthos living in London for years and studying the history of his home island. He has also written a number of articles on Vesalius. You should meet him.'

So far a simple message – but is the background just as simple? Zakynthos indeed is not large; everyone knows everyone, but did the neighbour of … truly tip off the mother of … – or did it go the other way round?

Still today Pavlos Plessas enriches his blog with the little and big history of his native island under a pseudonym. He says he does so because he wants to stay independent of local conditions and circumstances. Today he is still independent, but now everyone in Zakynthos knows who is signing off as Pampalaios and it would please me to think that I have something to do with it.

'There is even a street named after your family,' I wrote to him once after one of my wanderings through the city. 'The street is named after the archbishop,' he replied. 'The family is from the centre of the island, at the foot of the mountains. The first ones came here five hundred years ago, from the Pelopponese, after the invasion of the Turks. A clan fled to Sicily and became the Plescia. In Zakynthos we are about a few hundred today, a few in Athens and elsewhere. We have always been described as "hillbillies" (not without reason), but some have excelled in the church, politics or art (icons).'

After the aforementioned tip off, I read as a first text on the blog this contribution in which I could decipher the words 'Belgium' and 'Vesalius'. The blog was quite harsh. I didn't make the connection with the 'hillbilies', but I found his opinion to be as blunt and as honest as it was direct. And after a second reading, I really liked it.

'Translating that blog of mine is no mean feat. It contains a lot of Greek football idioms and words borrowed from the Zakynthos dialect and history. You must have had some help!'

> 'The Belgians have never been very eager to find or investigate the circumstances of [Vesalius's] death and his tomb. If they assumed that his grave was in Laganas, why then have they never searched for it? And if they were not sure, why have they done nothing to become certain. Why didn't they look after this abandoned area? Do they have any information about what happened in the fall of 1564? Did they properly analyze and study this? Not at all, I tell you. I cannot say why I think so, but I can give you an idea.

Imagine that you know someone really well and you know that he is in good health, and then he dies on the South Pole. Would you not ask yourself whether or not he died from the cold, especially since there is a witness who says that he showed signs of hypothermia? Or will you accept the testimony that a polar bear has slain him, knowing well that there are no polar bears at the South Pole.

If the Belgians had done their work and given their attention to the memorial, it would not have disappeared. Of course the people of Zakynthos would have helped Vesalius. Half of the literature on the death of Vesalius says that the islanders let him die of hunger. The other half takes no position on the matter. The fact is that the death of Vesalius was never good publicity for the island. No one has done more harm than this liar of a jeweller (who has spread the fiction of his death in a shipwreck on a deserted beach). [Of this we will hear more in Chapter 15]. We may have our bad sides, but we would never let a man die of hunger. And now we are supposed to feel guilty, and ashamed to admit that the stone is gone. As Belgium is a small fish, Greece too is a dot on the map; not only will we be able to say where Vesalius is buried, we will even find the cause of his death. I hope the committee that the mayor has convened has a doctor among them, because one will be needed. In any case, at the end of the story we will raise a glass to the Belgians because they have thrown the ball back in our camp, and that's important.'

It was immediately clear, we needed this man on our side. On Saturday, May 5, 2012 Pascale Pollier contacted him: 'Would you be interested in collaborating on our research project? Would it be possible to meet to discuss this in some greater depth? We feel your personal knowledge of the history of Zakynthos is invaluable to our research. I live in London and could make myself available at any time.'

A few hours later, Pavlos responded, flattered but modest: 'But then how could I describe your invitation to join your research project? The truth is I find it a little daunting but at the same time its aims are so exciting that I could not possibly refuse. I am afraid though you have overestimated my knowledge of Zakynthos history. I am neither a scholar nor is my knowledge great, systematic or comprehensive. I became involved in this quite accidentally, and I may not be able to contribute in the slightest to your project. I am, however, fully behind you in what you are trying to achieve and if you feel I can assist in some way I am ready to try.'

Later still, not even twenty-four hours after the first message, the partnership was sealed: 'Omer Steeno, Maurice Biesbrouck and Theodoor Goddeeris (....), in their latest article, have referred to your blog and would like your full name so they can credit you in their publication.'

That is how the road of the three Flemish experts and local croniqueur have touched and crossed. Meetings would follow soon, first in London, then on Zakynthos, later in Leuven and Antwerp.

14. Vesalius Momentum II: Zakynthos

Andreas Vesalius
Flandriae primus filius
Eminentissimus medicus
Hominis anatomicus

Andreas van Wesele
Hy whas veurwaer gheen eesele
Hy studheerde medicynen
's weirelts beste der chirurgynen

Drei was nen echten Brusseleir
Dane ket snei mè zaain gruëte scheir
As doktaur van de noblesse
In 't vel van prinse en prinsesse
André Van Wezel was zijn naam

Hij was een Vlaam met wereldfaam,
Maar na 't schrijven van zijn boek
Raakte hij op een eiland zoek

This satirical poem in Latin and several variants of Dutch,
by Em. Prof.dr. Dirk Lahaye cannot be translated properly.
I only paraphrase the last lines:
'Once written his book, he got lost on the island where we now look'.

In *A. Vesalius* journal of the medical alumni of KU Leuven, yr 26, p. 42, 2014.
The piece is illustrated by a picture of the famous Blue Caves of Zakynthos.

Upon hearing the name of Zakynthos, many immediately think of the famous postcard of a shipwreck on an azure bay, enclosed by steep cliffs. Partly thanks to this iconic image, the Ionian island has become very popular in recent years. With this romantic view on the postcard, the island makes a great effort to overcome the libertine reputation it has been given, especially in the United Kingdom, where 'Zante, bloody Zante' is still synonymous with 'sand, sea, sun and sex.' In the Vesal district in the Laganas Bay, there is a strip of bars and nightclubs that in the UK is popularly also called 'Slaganas'.

In recent years the beach tourism comes increasingly from Eastern Europe. Eco-tourism and cultural tourism, which the island deserves much more of, is difficult to get off the ground.

The fact that direct charter flights from the rest of Western and Eastern Europe have expanded a great deal recently, has helped though. In June 2013, 655 charter flights landed with nearly 100,000 passengers, which is an increase of over 12 per cent compared to 2012.

Thanks to a direct flight from and to Belgium, the proportion of Belgians who visit the island has, since 2013, increased a great deal. At this point in time Belgian compatriots already make up 2 per cent of all visitors to the globally popular island. In these statistics, coach and ferry passengers are not included.

Anyone visiting the island, drives, at least once, to see the famous shipwreck on the Navagio beach, which is by the north-western village of Elation. Others reach the iron skeleton from the sea, a trip that can only be made by boats from Porto Vromi, Volimes or on shuttle boats from Zakynthos and other touristic places. Many tourists depart from these same places on a perilous trip by quad, sometimes in caravan. During the busy summer months, local surgeons are always very busy patching up these unwary tourists. The Embassy receives calls every year from the islands, with the request that we inform the families at home of such a trip turned bad, and when and how the unfortunate drivers should be brought home.

If the inexperienced, and usually half naked, drivers, on their high-powered and unstable machines have managed to reach their destination alive, they face another danger. They have to struggle past stalls full with local products. I do not know if these small markets with their local wine, honey, jam and candy are a major contributor to the local economy, but there are not too many other facilities over there. The neighbourhood gives a sloppy impression.

Most people, however, come just for the adventure of walking onto the small viewing platform. Not so long ago this bridge must have had an extension that went a little further into the void, but part of it has now been sawn off. Photographing tourists must now tilt perilously over the edge to capture on their smart phone the rusty beast that lies down on the beach.

After ten minutes, they venture back to their hotel. The black dots located below, crowding around the Panagiotis ship, must stay around for another hour or so in the sun, or swim in the sea, before the boats return. There is not much else to see but this rusty smuggling ship that foundered, with a cargo of illegal cigarettes from Turkey, in bad weather in 1982 and crashed on the rocks. There are no stalls down on the beach.

In 1995, the young Greek artist Ioannis Markopoulos ritually tied the wreck with ropes fixed to the landscape. He called his work 'Gulliver', after the hero of Jonathan Swift who was tied up by Lilliputians.

In an article in the newspaper *Ermis*, Katerina Demeti, on July 3, 2009, rhetorically raised the question, 'Does the artist suggest that we, like Lilliputians, stick to a rusty and dismantled smuggling boat, investing in tourism, rather than in beauty, nature, culture and the people who inhabit it?'

Some will find it necessary to immediately formulate this answer: 'Today on the cliff above the Navagio beach you can even do base jumping; the videos are on YouTube.'

The iconic image of the deserted beach of Zakynthos is false. Just as false as the concoction that Vesalius died in a shipwreck. Vesalius did not die shipwrecked.

In 2012, the French surgeon Jean-Paul Chigot in *Du Scalpel à la Plume* dared to write 'imagined memoirs', in the name of Vesalius while he is dying on a Greek beach. In the introduction, the French surgeon, novelist, and biographer of Vesalius addresses his readers: 'I took the liberty of doing it [writing his memoirs] in his place.' A few lines further, he forces his main character to agree, by admitting that he [Vesalius] cannot write: 'I handle the knife better than the pen.'

All alone on a desert island, as it seems, the great anatomist catches fish for his lunch, shellfish, eggs, and complains that he is fed up with olives and is almost out of fresh water. Unlike Tom Hanks in the movie *Castaway*, he is not saved (and not nominated for best actor either): after fifteen days of agony from an infected leg, Vesalius dies. Just before he died, however, Vesalius had completed his memoirs and hidden them in a cave. During the first pages of the book, a monk shows up, questioning Vesalius about an attempt to save the life of a sailor. That night Vesalius has a nightmare about the monk, who is torturing him. Just before his death on the island, Vesalius asks himself this last and ultimate question: the monk on the ship, is he the same as in my dream? (yes, he is, the writer presented him as such); did this monk follow him during his trip? (no, he did not, the writer didn't mention him again during the trip). Vesalius's final thought is: 'if he did follow me, it's good he drowned'. (Why is it good he died, he didn't follow, did he?)

In 2013 in Flanders, the historical novel *Vesalius* by Joris Tulkens lands on the bookshelves. I was abroad and the online bookstore had kept me in suspense for weeks. I eagerly asked the author by e-mail how Vesalius died in his novel. His answer: 'I have written the novel from the perspective of Vesalius himself, and so I find it hard to tell him about his own death.'

When I finally had the book in hand, I went straight to the epilogue: 'Upon his return, he is shipwrecked and he dies from hunger.'

Why do authors such as Tulkens and Chigot so stubbornly cling to the myth of the shipwreck? More puzzling is that medical historians and self-proclaimed Vesalius specialists keep the myth alive as well. How many times will the word shipwreck fall on the Vesalius Conference in September 2014?

Shipwrecks suggest that travellers, whether they were called Gulliver, cigarette smugglers or a scientist returning from a pilgrimage, failed to reach their destination and thus have had a miserable end.

Every good story should not only end in death, as I earlier quoted, and to this I add: to be very good the story must have a social and political background that transcends the actual story. I sail here on my feelings, but maybe someone should check who had a vested interest, and who still has, in perpetuating the idea that Vesalius had to die ingloriously in a shipwreck.

On July 18, 2012 I organized a second 'Vesalius Momentum' on Zakynthos, especially for those who had missed the first one in Athens. On the touristic beach hotel Zakantha in Argassi, just outside the city, which is only open during the summer months, I spent some time with my family on vacation. That is also why I tried to keep the meeting as informal as possible.

Under the beautiful pergola of red bougainvillea on this beach, fifty people gathered to attend the meeting. Panos Kolyris, the vice mayor of tourism represented the mayor; his secretary, my irreplaceable contact at the municipallity, was there; and furthermore Kostas Gelades, the Chairman of the Council of Pantokratores, Katerina Demeti of the Solomos and Kalvos Museum, Pavlos Plessas and his wife (also on vacation), Dr. Kapsambelis and his son, and Maria Voulstou and her husband.

To the great surprise of all, Maria Voulstou was introduced as a spokesperson for the Medical Association, which was preparing the Vesalius Conference on Zakynthos. The charming Maria Voulstou is a pharmacist. Commenting on my welcome speech, Kapsambelis reacted also with the message that we Belgians should engage in the artistic aspect of the event, but that the medical conference would be coordinated from the universities of Patras and Corfu. It was not immediately clear to me that I, as coordinator of the Vesalius Continuum conference, was being casually pushed aside. In the television interview that was recorded and broadcast the next day, Maria Voulstou, the spokesperson, could only but translate my enthusiastic plans.

To this meeting, barely a few days before the Belgian national holiday, I had also invited a few compatriots. Indeed there are a few families that live on the island, but for others who do not, with the help of modern tourism, it is not so far away. The hotel owners informed me there was a Flemish couple who have stayed a fortnight at this hotel every year for the past twenty-five years. The representative of Jetair appeared to have links with the Belgian foreign affairs office and that turned out to be handy contact for in one or another consular file.

The friendship with two other families remains to this day, Livy Merchant and William Nagels. The former, who, as the son of an American Ambassador in Brussels became Belgian, recently moved to the Netherlands; since that meeting on Zakynthos, we keep in touch. I have recently enjoyed reading his latest book, *The Shades of Istanbul: A Novel with Ghosts,* a philosophical parable about an American professor, the Belgian owner of Hotel Antwerp in Istanbul, a Greek Gnostic monk and a Turkish Sufi, with an ecumenical happy ending whereby they live together in an old chapel on Zakynthos.

Here the Belgian businessman William Nagels also appears for the first time in the annals of the Vesalius Continuum. The initial contacts with Nagels date from a correspondence with Omer Steeno, but this fizzled out. Keen in being involved in the projects on Zakynthos the first of many meetings take place.

Unfortunately Pollier, Van de Velde and others of our committee could not be there on this occasion. For a while we had also expected that Ambassador Van de Reeck would join us from Athens, but he was at that moment on the way to Belgium, carrying in his luggage the painting by Peter Paul Rubens that Greek police had recovered a few months earlier in an undercover operation.

In our search for the tomb of Vesalius, this Momentum did not achieve a great deal. For the relations between the Committee of Vesalius Continuum and the Greek hosts and hostesses it was all the more significant. In some of the ties, irreparable cracks have since appeared, with others the tears healed up; some ties stayed weak, others strengthened, some for life.

Directly following the television broadcast on this Momentum, I was contacted by Panagiota Aktypi, the dynamic director of the First Lyceum of Zakynthos. In the company of some students, she came the very next day to the hotel. This meeting would eventually develop into a successful school exchange funded by the European Comenius Fund.

From 7 to 18 February 2014, a Greek class led by Aktypi, and accompanied by Maria Agriou (Greek teacher), Sofia-Eleni Parastatidou (art teacher), Dionysia Theodoritsi (biologist) and Christos Gousias (physics teacher), went to Heverlee.

From 27 March to 4 April, the Belgians, with Veerle Deserrano (vice-director), Linda Schilders and Gerda Somers (maths teachers), Det Rottie (form teacher of class 608), and Patricia Verbeke (Philhellenic and driving force behind the Belgian leg of the Comenius projects) went to Zakynthos.

In Greece they were warmly received by Efrosyni Lasou, Katherina Tsikrika and Lefkothea-Vasiliki Andreou (English teacher), who also translated and interpreted. Their videos, exhibitions, theatre play and trips and lessons prove that the dream of promoting Andreas Vesalius as a bridge builder in time and space has come true.

Between the first meeting with Panagiota Aktypi after the Momentum in July 2012 and today, a storm has raged in Zakynthos that finally blew the myth of the shipwreck off the table. I recall that Mrs Aktypi, at the start of the project, elaborated on a project about Homer and Zakynthos. I was not surprised. Two years later, I heard a speech about how the identity of the islanders is not only shaped by the classics, but also by coincidental passers-by as Vesalius. Then I *was* surprised. The students there are now more aware of the latest developments in Vesalius research than their parents, and many specialists.

The interest of these eighteen- and nineteen-year-olds is a life insurance for the permanent and correct memory of Andreas Vesalius. Obviously this does not come easily to everyone. When it appeared that the new theatre of Zakynthos would not be ready to be inaugurated by the Continuum Conference in September, the municipality and the Embassy were approached by lobby groups from the tourist area of Laganas. The conference hall of a five-star hotel was offered free of charge. It was suggested the new statue would be more in its natural environment there than in the city. 'Was it not your Vesalius who was cast upon a deserted place near Laganas in a storm?'

The tourist industry on the island has never played the card of Vesalius. The truth is that the idea that Vesalius died of hunger never was good publicity for the island, so says Pavlos Plessas. Now that the attention is shifting from Kalogerata/Laganas to the city and the idea that the world-renowned physician, writer and nobleman seems to be buried there, their attention is unfortunately too late.

15. The creaking of the ropes and the noise of camels

The theory that there was a shipwreck is now refuted by most researchers. 'Half of the literature on the death of Vesalius says that the islanders let him die of hunger. The other half does not take a position on the matter. The fact is that the death of Vesalius has never been good publicity for the island.'

Thus Pavlos Plessas continued to sum it up altogether.

> 'Only two eyewitness accounts of [Vesalius's] death exist … Perhaps the most widely known is that of the Italian Pietro Bizzari, based on what he was told by an anonymous Venetian goldsmith. The goldsmith claimed that he had happened upon the sick Vesalius by chance on a deserted beach and, in spite of the opposition Bizzari had faced from the Zakynthians, had tried to assist him in his final hours and had buried him with his own hands in a plot he had purchased for that purpose.
>
> The other account is that of the Frenchman Jean Matal, better known as Johannes Metellus, who was given the information by Georg Boucher, a German from Nuremberg. Boucher claimed he had met Vesalius in Egypt. Zakynthos was the first land they reached after a terrifying journey of forty days. As a result of food and water shortages, several persons on board the ship had fallen ill and some died. The famous anatomist, poorly supplied with provisions, fell ill, initially with worry over the breakout of the disease and his own fate. Soon after disembarking Vesalius dropped dead and Boucher arranged for a stone to be put on his grave.'

Very systematically, Pavlos Plessas then analyzes the story of Bizzari: 'Too vague because it includes no data or details about the location or circumstances; it is unlikely that a famous nobleman was left behind by fellow passengers; what about the attitude of the well-organized local government, contradicting testimonies of visitors who a little later visited the grave in the Santa Maria delle Grazie, etc.

The version of Metellus's about the sick Vesalius who dropped dead on the quayside is much more credible.

In the academic journal *Vesalius – Internationalia Acta Historiae Medicinae*, issued by the ISHM[1], appears the following article, which may not remain unread by any Vesalius specialist.

It builds on two previous articles in a series entitled 'The Last Months of Andreas Vesalius' and now receives from the authors Maurice Biesbrouck, Theodoor Goddeeris and Omer Steeno this addition to the title: 'A Coda'. The article follows their discovery of two yet unfamiliar texts about the death and burial of Vesalius. Hidden, so to speak, in a book by Thomas Theodor Crusius, they found a report on the death of Vesalius by Reinerus Solenander, German author who also studied medicine in Leuven. The letter is dated May 1566, which is less than two years after the death of anatomist.

Until its formal publication in the *Official Journal of the International Society for the History of Medicine*, I had to promise them solemnly that I would handle this very interesting material discreetly. Now, after its publication, it would be criminal of me not to present this text, discovered by Goddeeris in the library of Wolfenbüttel, to a more general public. The English translation of the letter in Latin, with a short introduction in German, I take literally from the article by Steeno, Biesbrouck and Goddeeris:

> 'As I wish to give a brief report of the death and burial of the famous doctor and anatomist Andreas Vesalius, I should also recount something of the story of his life. But as others including Adam and Freher have already written on this matter, I do not so much wish to repeat their facts here as merely to keep a promise and give an account of Vesalius which differs in various places from that of the said authors, and which likewise flowed from the pen of a doctor of learning and renown; that account runs as follows:

Account of the death of Andreas Vesalius
according to the letter of Reinert Solenander
during the Diet of Augsburg, May 1566

Vesalius left Spain with his wife and travelled to Marseilles, in order to depart for Palestine. Whether he did this out of religious conviction or for the sake of profit I cannot adequately discern. I believe that it was not for religious reasons, for he never attached any importance to religion. In Holland and the surrounding regions there are many who travel there for profit, and it was the custom to do thus: those who made this journey had everything with them and would lend it out at interest, on the understanding that if one gave a person one-fold, one would receive back two-fold or more when he came back, but if he failed to come back he and his family would lose their property. When he came to Marseilles, his wife had already left him: she had previously quarrelled with her husband and refused to go any further with him. After their separation, she left for Belgium, and Vesalius continued on his way to Venice, as I understand, without having been reconciled with his wife.

After embarking there, he sailed for Jerusalem and wandered around those parts. Once all his travel companions had visited everything there, they returned by ship. Initially, owing to stormy weather, they were driven off course, and when they had been driven into the open sea the air became so peaceful (one might rather say "the wind was stilled"), that the ship drifted around for several weeks in virtually the same place. It was high summer and baking hot. Then most of the passengers fell ill, and many died. When he saw them being thrown into the sea for several days in succession, Vesalius became dispirited and began to suffer from sickness himself, but did not say anything about it. While they were drifting around in the same spot in this way, the provisions began to run out. There was a general shortage and a severe lack of drinking water. A daily ration was given to each, but beyond that – as an emergency reserve – not a drop more than was deemed necessary. Having ended up in this desperate situation, Vesalius, who was taciturn by nature, melancholy and not provided for such an eventuality, received no care, as the necessary provisions had by now run out, and he started to become more seriously ill. When he, a sick person himself, had to watch fellow passengers being thrown overboard day after day, he went to implore the captain and other crew members not to throw him too into the sea should anything happen to him or should he die. After they had been drifting around for a long time, the wind finally began to pick up and they were able to sail on with a favourable wind. In the meantime, Vesalius lay sick in the hold and had nobody to encourage him or tend to him. When land was sighted, everyone became frenzied, but he became even more seriously ill. Only then did the travellers arrive at Zakynthos; they called to him and when they entered the port and struck sail, Vesalius expired amid the creaking of the ropes and the noise of camels. But he obtained what he had most desired, namely that he should be carried ashore and buried on land, near a chapel or shrine near the port of Zakynthos.

This story was told by a merchant from Nuremberg, who had embarked together with Vesalius in Venice. When they [on their outward journey] arrived in Cyprus, the merchant left his fellow travellers there and departed for Alexandria aboard another ship. From there he travelled to Cairo, and then, after completing his business, returned and in Cyprus, by a great coincidence, rejoined the same ship and the same travel companions [on their return journey]. Once he had rejoined them, he too underwent these dangers and experienced the same fate as his fellow travellers. After he had left Vesalius on Zakynthos and buried him, he returned to Venice, however. After his wife had learnt of the death of her husband, she quickly married another, a certain nobleman. Vesalius left his daughter the sum of twelve thousand thalers and an annual income of more than seven hundred.

Vesalius, the supreme glory of our art,
died at sea, and his grave lies in Zakynthos.
In the year 1564.

§ 2. Those who claim that our Vesalius perished in a poor fisherman's hut on the island of Zakynthos, whither he had been driven from Cyprus by a storm, are therefore mistaken. But I leave it open to question whether it was the idea of the merchant from Nuremberg, whom others claim was a goldsmith, to provide his grave with the following inscription:

"GRAVE OF ANDREAS VESALIUS OF BRUSSELS,
DIED ON 15 OCTOBER 1564
AT THE AGE OF 58 YEARS,
AS HE WAS RETURNING FROM JERUSALEM"

More later about the precise burial place, but concerning the cause of death of Vesalius, the three authors conclude their article with two thoughts I absolutely have to present here too:

'At the moment of disembarkation at Zakynthos, Vesalius must have physiologically crossed the 'red line', the point at which the provision of fluid and calories would have come too late to make up for the already irreparable damage to his severely weakened constitution. He did not die as a result of shipwreck, illness, but from sheer hardship. Thus he was not 'cast onto the rocks' as some romantic depictions later showed.'

'We strongly suspect that the merchant from Nuremberg (Solenander), Georges Boucher from Nuremberg (Metellus/Matal) and the mysterious goldsmith (Bizarri) are one and the same person, so that each of these authors tells part of the true story, albeit supplemented with some fabricated details – from hearsay or by tradition – to fill the gaps.'

On his blog Pavlos Plessas responds almost immediately on the appearance of the article of those 'men who have for many years engaged in the study of the life and work of Vesalius and are rightly considered authorities on the subject'.

In fact, he analyzes the last thought of the Belgians in greater detail:

'Solenander's letter, as he says himself, is based on the testimony of a merchant from Nuremberg, just like the known letters of Metellus, in one of which the merchant is named as Georgius Boucherus.

It is, however, obvious that Solenander's text is not based on those letters since he mentions additional information, like the location of the grave, and at the same time has differences, for example that Vesalius breathed his last on board the ship. This does not necessarily mean that Solenander did not know Metellus's version and did not incorporate some of its elements in the one he presented. Especially his hypothesis of the financial motive of the pilgrimage and the possible bet may have their roots in what Metellus had been promulgating.

(…)

The importance of this evidence though is huge and does not stop here. Its initial source was Boucherus, effectively this is what Solenander tells us. So Boucherus is placed in Zakynthos, at the time of Vesalius's funeral, or a little later at the most. It is known that Vesalius died in mid-October and Levant travellers tried to return before the onset of winter. Besides, by next spring Boucherus had already narrated his story to Metellus and Doctor Echtius in Germany. Part of this story is that Vesalius expected a large sum of money upon his return. This forms part of the story that Solenander recounts too. Vesalius being owed money is a fact that we also derive from elsewhere (…). The only way, however, that a German merchant travelling in the Levant could know what arrangements Vesalius had made in Spain before his departure was to have been told by Vesalius himself. If a man travelling to Egypt met someone who had gone to Palestine, and they got familiar enough to discuss their finances, then this could mean only one thing: that they travelled together. So, we have in front of us the proof that Boucherus was telling the truth.

With regards to the differences of Solenander's version with that of Metellus, the latter's must be considered more reliable since it comes from a face-to-face conversation with Boucherus. It is not known how many people came between Boucherus and Solenander. For this reason Vesalius's death on board the ship must be considered inaccurate, while for his meeting with Boucherus in Venice and their coincidence in Cyprus we can be justifiably sceptical. Besides, the chances that the same ship waited for the pilgrims for three months or that she went back to pick them up are minimal. Also their stay in the Holy Land for three whole months is not easily explainable when most pilgrims did not stay for more than two or three weeks, especially as, according to Metellus, Vesalius was in a hurry to return. It is probably an effort by Solenander, or one of his informants, to reconcile how Vesalius, for whom he knew only that he visited Palestine, met with Boucherus, who was travelling from Egypt. It is worth noting that Metellus, a known cartographer with excellent knowledge of geography and whom Boucherus would have acquainted with Vesalius's itinerary, did not feel the need to offer an explanation.

(…)

The other piece of information, given much more clearly than in Metellus's texts, is that the victims of the mysterious disease that killed Vesalius were his travelling companions and not the crew of the ship. This excludes the possibility that the disease was contagious or that Vesalius may have died from hunger, thirst and the hardships of the journey – the hard-working sailors would have been far more susceptible to those than the passengers. It shows that the causes of the disease must be sought in the conditions that Vesalius and his companions faced before, or even long before, they boarded the ship. In that respect it strengthens the theory that Vesalius died from scurvy, which occurred after many months of travel, both in the sea and in desert and semi-desert areas, during the hottest months of the year (…).'

Even if the Belgian authors of the Coda article say that 'in our view, Vesalius did not die of the consequences of scurvy, as Pavlos (Plessas) suggests', it is true that a lack of vitamin C or ascorbic acid, which is the cause of the illness, was a frequent problem among seafarers at that time. But the Mediterranean region is generally safeguarded against it, owing to its abundance of citrus fruits and other fruits rich in vitamin C. Moreover, the period of forty days during which the ship was adrift was far too short to cause symptoms.

Pavlos Plessas again immediately took up the challenge and developed a new post on his blog as a proof that not only the trip itself, but the entire stay in the Holy Land was not very good for Vesalius's physical health, as opposed to his spiritual health, I might add.

16. Holy Mary of Grace

'Just outside the city lies a mansion that was once owned by a prominent English-Zakynthian family, the Sargints. After a stay of centuries in Zakynthos, they left the island when the Axis powers marched in. Today, the villa is owned by the Catholic Church. It seems that stones have been saved there from the St Mark's Church dating from long before the earthquake. Here is a picture; I do not know what it is. I'm still trying to figure out whether there is still anything else in the villa. Because we can't leave any stone unturned, can we?'

In the photo attached, a huge block of pink marble, at least two metres long, one metre high and a bit wider, and on the front a gracefully sculpted scene of floral patterns and a beautiful central sculpture of two crossed arms. In a V formed by the forearms, there is the damaged image of what looks like a cross, but part of the image is cut away with force.

Pavlos Plessas sent the above message to me in early July 2012.

During the second Momentum in Zakynthos we agreed with him and the diabolical trio that, during the summer, we would check more traces of Vesalius on the terrain. My vacation in July would be particularly intense.

In order to make those weeks bearable for my family, trips to the rest of the island were made between visits to real and false resting placings. It should be said that on these trips many abbeys and monasteries were visited, in the hopes that I would stumble upon the sixteenth century, the Franciscans and Vesalius.

Even though this quest came down by detective work to the Santa Maria delle Grazie, or remnants thereof, in an area we knew quite well, the stone with the crossed arms stands for much more than a mere single stone.

The web of emails that we have woven, in preparation for this trip, say as much about the enthusiasm with which we have sought the grave as about the disappointment in tracing its disappearance and the suspicion and rivalry that continues.

Pavlos Plessas is cautious. Even though he has lived and worked for most of his life in London, he knows his native island like the inside of his pockets. His blog is read, but he keeps himself away from the personalities of the island. I have introduced him to many of them myself. It's been already more than obvious that he had a solid informant. He is always immediately aware of press articles; he regularly receives tips about action on the ground. So he knew faster than anyone else that works had started at the corner of Kolokotroni and Kolyva. The discovery of this stone is another example. Who was behind his expression 'it seems that…' and how he would try to 'figure it out' was not immediately clear from this first mail.

In a subsequent message he says that the stone was discovered by Maria Sidirokastriti who also had taken the picture. Author of a travelling guide to Zakynthos, explorer of every corner of the island, friend of every islander, her charm is applauded. He did not say how she had managed to enter the mansion, but 'according to Maria the stone lies in front of the villa which is usually unoccupied. Only during the summer some people come visiting. She does not know whether elsewhere in the site or in the house still lie hidden pieces. But it might be worthwhile to ask if we could possibly be allowed to look around and possibly take more pictures.'

About the crossed over arms in stone, of which I did not know what they represent, I consulted Jan Driessen, Director of the EBSA, who soon heard from an Italian colleague that the image of the crossed arms on the stone link the stigmata of Christ with those of St Francis, and that it often occurs in Franciscan churches. About the period, he only said that the stone is probably from the 17th century.

I then wrote to Spiros Gaoutsis, my fellow Consul of Malta, the Secretary of the Catholic Archbishop of Corfu, who was introduced to me by Omer Steeno. Does the villa belong to the church? Does he know if there are more stones or pieces lying around? Are we allowed to visit the villa? Is there nothing refering to Vesalius?

This is his answer on June 14, 2012:

> 'The villa that you describe is actually owned by the Catholic Diocese of Zakynthos. It was the residence of Robert Sargint, (…). The building is damaged beyond repair. I had heard of the stone with the Franciscan symbol that you have shown me. In the garden there are the ruins of an ancient chapel. The piece could be the Santa Maria delle Grazie, although that was not the only Franciscan church in Zakynthos. If after earthquakes pieces were also collected with reference to Vesalius, I do not know.
>
> During your stay, please contact Reverend S.T., a monk who speaks Italian, or Ms Mercy P., concierge. This is her phone number.'

Slightly disappointed that Gaoutsis does not elaborate on the Franciscan properties on the island, Pavlos Plessas is nonetheless pleased with the agreement and together we look forward to our visit. Immediately afterwards I receive his request: Can Maria join us? Of course she can. This is the world upside down: local guides approach me and ask to join.

On Tuesday, July 17, we meet at St Mark's Church in the city, between the Solomos Museum and Hotel Diana in Metropoleus Street. That is where Mercy P. works and also helps in the Catholic Church next door. She sends her flamboyant husband along as guide to the villa. We have made an appointment with Maria, who lives nearby. On the locked iron gate, this sign: Catholic Archdiocese of Corfu, Zakynthos and Kefalonia; juvenile colony of Saint Mark.

The leafy terrain lies high above Zakynthos between hills with upmarket villas. Just past the entrance are the sunken ruins of a chapel. The stone rests between the dilapidated villa and some annexed buildings on the edge of the mountain, on steel bars. While Plessas and I scour the land for other relics of the church, the husband of Mercy delivers a speech on what this villa could muster as a tourist destination. With great difficulty, we convince him to view the villa inside: no electricity, barely light, some bunk beds, lots of debris, but absolutely no stones or other references to the church.

When and how this heavy stone was placed here is not clear; the Catholic and Franciscan origins are obvious though. But where did other, more easily transportable, remnants of the destroyed church go? To other properties of the diocese? Possibly with the Sargints?

On December 10, Claire, the daughter of Robert Sargint, responds to my question about that. She thanks me for the information. With references to the website of Vesalius Continuum and my Facebook page, she wishes us good luck with Vesalius on Zakynthos. In a few sentences, she looks at a New Year's card that I had forwarded from the Solomos Museum with a floral drawing of her grandfather, Anastasius Sargint. The museum indeed owns a collection of drawings of flowers and other albums with views of Zakynthos, donated by her father to the Solomos Museum, and another in the National Museum of Athens. The drawing of the hospital that I had sent was indeed from her father, she says, but if a drawing of the Santa Maria delle Grazie exists, she does not know. 'Good luck with your plans, I follow you on your website.'

On the way back from the villa to the city, I showed Pavlos Pavlos the tombstones that lie behind St Mark's Church. I had discovered them during a previous visit and already knew they did not contain a reference to Vesalius.

A few months later, in a short report to Spiros Gaoutsis, I carefully write this PS: 'As usual, I went again to check whether the beautiful tombstones still lie behind the church, and what a relief, they are still there. Do you happen to know from who is the depicted coat of arms?'

Answer on May 16, 2013: 'The picture of the remains of the old St Mark make me sad. I have not been for years in Zakynthos and I'm sorry that you have to see that. Despite urging the Archbishop, there is no one to save the monuments or restore them. That's just the fate of a church that has no permanent priest. The coat of arms is that of Bishop Francesco Mercati.'

In the following weeks I try to convince both Gaoutsis Spiros and Katerina Demeti, seperately, to lend the tombstones to the Solomos Museum next door. They would be safe there and could be admired by many visitors. Both think it is a good idea: Gaoutsis will ask the Archbishop, Demeti will ask the advisory board of the museum.

During my most recent visit to St Mark's Church in February 2014 the tombstones of the Venetian nobleman Francesco Mercati, who from 1785 to 1803 was Bishop of Kefalonia and Zakynthos, were... gone.

17. From the low lands

Andreas Vesalius was nineteen when he went to Paris to study medicine at the university there. His teachers were Jacobus Sylvius and Johannes Gunterius Andennacus. Influenced at first by Sylvius, Vesalius was inspired by the theories of the great classical Greek anatomist Galen (131–201 AD), without much objection from his side.

To increase his knowledge of the human body, he stole cadavers from the Parisian execution site Montfaucon and the then main cemetery of the French capital, le Cimetière des Saints Innocents.

In *Public Anatomy* from which I quoted in the opening of this book about the missing Vesalius, author Scott Pearson writes that the anatomist, 'while in Paris (on his way) to Montfaucon, (passes) the Cemetery of the Innocents', on which subject,

Illus. 10: Stealing cadavers in the initial letter L on plate 38 of de Fabrica of Vesalius.

I would like to add, Andrew Miller dedicated in 2011 an entire novel: *Pure*. Situated in the 18th century, Miller doesn't mention Vesalius at all, but rarely have I read such a beautiful love story about a graveyard. I'm not alone in thinking that this book surpasses Patrick Süskind's more famous *Perfume*.

Searching for the Cimetière des Saints Innocents makes little sense today, however. *Pure* tells how the cemetery near Les Halles was evacuated and the bones moved to the catacombs. Fortunately Maurice Biesbrouck wrote an essay in July 2012, in which he demonstrates how important the cemetery was for Vesalius. There I read that Vesalius once had to run for his life into Montfaucon, fleeing from a pack of wild dogs. He was accompanied on his rampages by his classmate, Matthew Terminus. He discovered that the human mandible is made from a single bone, in contrast to Galen's claims. The relationship with his teacher, Sylvius, was beginning to sour.

Due to the outbreak of the war between France and the Holy Roman Empire, Vesalius was forced, in 1536, to return to the Netherlands and Leuven.

There off the fish market, hidden behind a gate, is a blind alley called the Busleydengang. It is as if you are stepping back into the time of Vesalius. On the right, against the red brick, a grey plaque informs us that here stood the Collegium Trilingue:

College of Three Languages, founded in 1517 on the initiative of Erasmus by Hiëronymus Busleyden for the study of Latin, Greek and Hebrew

and

Buildings from 1517–1520 and 1612
Brick and sandstone architecture, original staircase tower
In the 19th century transformed into industrial buildings

With the founding of the Collegium Trilingue, Erasmus indeed executes the will of Jeroen van Busleyden. Erasmus became councellor of the Emperor Charles V in 1516 and settled in Leuven in Brabant.

It is there that Vesalius, during his first period in Leuven, studied the classical languages. He was fourteen when he arrived in Leuven for the first time, on February 25, 1530. From Maurice Biesbrouck I know that he learned his excellent Latin from Conradus Goclenius and Greek from Rutgerus Rescius. That his teacher, John Campensis, was equally pleased with his pupil remains uncertain: some found Vesalius's knowledge of Hebrew to be weaker.

When he returned to Leuven in 1536 to continue his medical studies, the Trilingue College was at the peak of its attainments and in its heyday.

Maurice Biesbrouck and Omer Steeno have just written another fascinating article with 'an impression of the year of 1537'. They bring to the research a lot more details of the emergence, flowering and final closure of the Collegium. They tell how Vesalius searched with his friend, Gemma Phrysius, for corpses, which they brought from the gallows into the city. He built his first skeleton. They also describe the study itinerary of an aspiring doctor in those years.

Vesalius was registered with the Pedagogium Castri, today located in Mechelsestraat. At that time there were four such schools or pedagogies; in Medicine, Canon Law, Civil Law and Theology. The schools were known as; Lilium/Lily, Porcus/Pig, Falcon/Falco and Castri/Borcht. Besides the anatomist, a number of prominent figures of that time graduated: Gerardus Mercator, the man who mapped the world, Perronet Antoine de Granvelle, future European statesman, and Georg Cassander, theologian and humanist.

In early 1537 Vesalius graduated with a thesis on 'Paraphrasis in nonum Librum Rhazae' [Comments on the ninth book of Rhazes], a commentary on a book by the great Arab physician Muhammad ibn Zakariya Razi, known as Rhazes.

In May 2012 I corresponded with the Dutch scientist and artist Abdul Haq Compier. On our website, under 'curiosities', I referred to his study of Vesalius and Rhazes. But he preferred not to be published under that title because 'the scope of the article is correct that Rhazes played an important role in the thinking of Vesalius'. He even suggested adding this quote: 'Vesalius' biographers have always regarded the start of his academic career with Rhazes a mere curiosity. Little did they take note that Vesalius also ended his career with an affirmation of sympathy for the Arabian author. (...) Vesalius developed an internationalist vision as he approached the decisive moment when empiricism was allowed to triumph over authority. (...) This liberation towards an international vision of science, I hope, will only add to the charm of the champion of Renaissance anatomy.'"

Andreas Vesalius left Leuven quite suddenly in March 1537. We have shown previously how Compier stressed the free and international aspirations of Vesalius. In the article just cited, Biesbrouck and Steeno also examine the reasons for his sudden departure. In a sense, they move in the same direction. They wonder whether his departure might have to do with the appointment of a reputed inquisitor rector of the university. In one of his letters, Vesalius alludes to the changing climate. Is that what triggered his departure? That alone or together with the appeal of Padua, which offered an excellent medical training? Or was it the French invasion of Flanders that brought him to new horizons, where he could develop himself in all liberty?

18. Vesalius Momentum III: Leuven

The third Vesalius Momentum meeting couldn't possibly have taken place any place other than in Leuven. After the initial Momentum, which took place on April 21, 2012 in Athens, the second had been held in July 18, 2012 in Zakynthos. Now, for this third meeting, co-financed by BIOMAB, I invited to Leuven, for 20–21 October, 2012 the now international company who make up the Vesalius Continuum: Maurits Biesbrouck, Eleanor Crook, Danielle Dergent, Marc De Roeck, Theodoor Goddeeris, Bryan W. Green, Pavlos Plessas, Pascale Pollier, Omer Steeno, Ann Van de Velde and Francis Van Glabbeek. On the second day came Jan Driessen, director of the EBSA and professor at UCL and Robert Van Hee, Prof. Em. History of Medicine, and they were joined by Jan Gielis and Stefan Van Langendonck, who are representatives of international medical students' associations. This meeting took place at the budget Ibis Hotel.

Those who think that international conferences only take place in five-star hotels, in exotic places are mistaken. The meagre budget that Vesalius Continuum works with, stands in stark contrast to the enthusiasm of its members. For me, some playfulness, irony, symbolism and most of all, a lot of friendship compensate for the difference.

The aperitif was taken in the legendary student bar, The Blue Barge, at the fish market. In my younger days I spent far too much time in this pub, which takes its name from the carnival jester's ship of the Middle Ages, and I undoubtedly contributed considerably to the fortunes of the owners.

The dinner was served in the Spanish-styled restaurant The Dry Tongues, the name of which is borrowed from old local colloquial terms referring to the three languages of the Trilingue Collegium. Immediately to the right of the restaurant is the spiral staircase that Vesalius would once have climbed and an ancient window through which one can see where Vesalius must have passed by.

The late night was later spent, with the international guests, in The Cosmopolitan Cafe, at the station. How else could it be?

Over the two days we discussed the various aspects of our plans, some of which were already established at this point, and are now nearly consolidated, almost unchanged, while others have already taken place. An exhibition of artworks of prominent medical and scientific artists, 'Fabrica Vitae', which Pollier and Eleanor Crook are organizing, will begin to travel. Early designs about the commemorative monument to mark the 2014 events in Zakynthosv are disclosed. The support of, and cooperation with, the heraldic specialist Theodoor Goddeeris to advise Chantal Pollier, who is creating the plinth of the monument, was agreed upon during this Momentum.

The most beautiful moments were captured on camera, and, against the backdrop of a grounded blue barge, Pavlos Plessas and Theodoor Goddeeris, bent over maps, are seen wondering whether the exact situation of the Santa Maria delle Grazie can be verified by reference to information from the 16th century. The place where their attention is now focused does not coincide in fact with that of 1564. After the meeting Pavlos put the detailed information on his blog when he received a copy of the Gentilini map of 1632 from the British Library. This map was also used for the GIS.

The discussions during the gambas a la plancha at the Dry Tongues were lighter, so I explained that I had previously considered two different locations for the meeting: the Egmont Palace on the Sablon and the Lyceum of Robert Catteau, both a stone's throw from the birthplace of Vesalius in Brussels, but sadly they were not available during the weekends.

Vesalius bibliophile Francis Van Glabbeek described various editions of the *Fabrica* with understated passion, comparing the different editions. He generously invited us to see and feel the originals, which he has in his private collection. He also spoke about the *Epistulae*, the letters of Vesalius.

Danielle Dergent, who is a musical historian specializing in music at the time of Vesalius, enlightened us about the importance of the vocal music of the period.

We were also trying to find ways to join together the conference in Zakynthos with cultural trips to other places where Vesalius passed by; but these trips are now leading an independent life steered by the Medical Journal and a travel agency.

This Momentum has, from all points of view, been a turning point in the search for the tomb. Until now the quest was carried out with great enthusiasm by 'a group from Antwerp, who are members of BIOMAB', as the Coda article of Omer Steeno and co states.

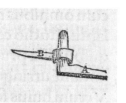

Illus. 11:
A turning point: the hinge on plate 44 of the Fabrica of Vesalius.

From now on, Pavlos Plessas and 'the group of Leuven', formally join the quest for the grave by Vesalius Continuum. Furthermore, both groups agree that the quest would be through official and professional channels only.

Precisely with this in mind, I had invited the EBSA director Jan Driessen and Pavlos Plessas from Zakynthos. Those from Antwerp – and from Leuven – would further refine their research papers and maps from libraries, but now it was time to complement their knowledge with data from the field.

The Greek Archaeology Act 2002 is clear: only the KAS (the Kentriko Archaiologikó Simvoulio), which is the Central Archaeological Committee, may decide on archaeological research in Greece and it presides over all proposals submitted, from the bottom to the top and about the large and major projects it manages itself. Local departments of the Ministry of Culture, called *eforias* can introduce proposals to the KAS or can transfer those of third parties. Concerning projects from foreign schools, the specialized DIPKA service of the Ministry of Culture has to be consulted.

Since the mid-nineteenth century foreign institutes have been recognized and permitted to do archaeological research in Greece. In the sixties, the Ghent professor Herman Mussche opened the door for the Belgians at the site of silver mines at Lavrion Thorikos. Step by step, his work and that of some others included in the activities of the Belgian School, has ensured that Belgium is now one of nearly twenty foreign institutes that work in Greece. Christiane Tytgat, whom we previously encountered at the Athens Momentum, was the first director. She was succeeded by Steven Soetens, who in turn was replaced by Jan Driessen, who plays a role in this adventure. Panagiotis Iossef is the driving force in Athens.

'Foreign schools' are official institutions recognized by the Greek government as sole interlocutors. The various universities, in our case Louvain, Liège and Ghent, are considered, by Greek Archaeological Department, as teams of the Belgian School, the EBSA. Universities may, under exceptional circumstances, work together with local and *eforia* proposals, but the *eforia* are always in charge. Ongoing and new projects must be submitted by 30 November each year. The decisions of the local services, the Ministry of Culture and the KAS are taken in relation to the proposed dates for the following year of work.

That's the theory. In practice we are still far from digging.

As the spot where we situate the Santa Maria delle Grazie is an urban and built-up environment, non-destructive archaeological research methods had to be instigated initially. Thus I had to announce, in my introduction, that a first contact with the University of Ghent was not immediately successful.

A few weeks earlier, on September 18, 2012, I had seen, on TV, a news report about a soil survey around Stonehenge, the famous megalithic monument near Salisbury, in England. Ghent soil scientists employed a rolling soil sensor towed by a quad to investigate the plain around the mythical stone circle. Scientists from the Department of Soil Management at the University of Ghent, led by Professor Marc Van Meirvenne did so at the request of an international team of archaeologists. The

Research Spatial Soil Inventory Techniques (ORBit) of the Department of Soil of the Faculty of Bioscience Engineering, as described on their website, sound terribly scientific and difficult, but I had in my mind the image of the four-wheeler bikes riding around everywhere on Zakynthos. That was enough to give me hope that an appendage of Ghent would soon find the grave of Vesalius, without a shovel being stabbed into the ground, non-destructive as the professionals would say.

On October 3, 2012, I asked Professor Van Meirvenne, by email, if I could call him. In the message I included the links to the websites of Vesalius Continuum. The next day I recieved a friendly answer that we would need an archaeologist: 'I assume that you contact me on the basis of the media attention recently received by our activities in Stonehenge. As you could see in the programme our specialty is scanning large areas with a quad and we take on less detailed, manual searches of smaller sites, such as a burial cavity in a cemetery. If the latter is your intention, then I would suggest that you contact someone from archeology who performs such work with a radar.'

Professor Van Meirvenne suggested contacting a colleague archaeologist of his, from the University of Ghent.

I had already spoken extensively about our plans with Jan Driessen, so I put the suggestion to find an archaeologist with radar to the director of the Belgian School.

On June 10, 2012, he wrote: 'Ideally, we find a historian who is interested. As he wrote earlier: 'Such a project would normally be carried out by at least one or two Belgian professors.' Where ground exploration is concerned, there is indeed expertise in Ghent, but it can also be found in Greece itself. I work with Apostolos from Rethymnon. He is, however, difficult to get hold of, as are the funds needed for such an endeavour. Are you coming to Belgium in the near future?'

Thus it happened that I could announce, during the Momentum in Leuven, the new adventure of the official archaeological search for the grave. More explanations came from Jan Driessen who knows the Greek procedures like no other, though he was obviously dubious that the planned timing could be respected. It seemed that an initial investigation should be completed in the autumn of 2013, so that consent could be requested to dig in the spring of 2014, in order for it to be possible for the results to be presented in September 2014.

During this Momentum we also went looking for some other traces of Vesalius. We were sorry that the Anatomical Theatre at the park, was closed, because it was still leased as an art studio. Earlier I had been phoning and writing extensively, but we couldn't get in. And between the statues in the façade of the town hall of fame,

Mercator was discovered quite a bit faster than the somewhat hidden Vesalius. With the support of the tourist office and a catalogue of hundreds of the statues, we finally found the one who carries the number 144, around the corner of the Naamse Straat, the skull in his hand hardly recognizable.

19. To high ground

Young people go studying abroad, and this cannot happen soon enough these days. I have already boasted about our successful school exchange. It was soon clear to me that Andreas Vesalius mercilessly infects young people.

The Embassy of Belgium in Athens receives a lot of applications from youngsters requesting a place for a couple of week's internship. Usually, they are students who hope to learn more under the sun about international, and especially European, relations and institutions than in, say, the European Quarter in Brussels. They hope their diplomatic insights come more easily under a blue sky than beneath some of the greyer skies of the European states of the north and the east. Our colleagues in Spain and Italy, I assume, have a similar experience.

The young man who approached us in Greece during the summer of 2011 had eyes only for Greece. He wanted to be an archaeologist. I couldn't ask him to study the contemporary health sector of the country or to go deeper into the rather complex education system. I just asked him to dig up some Belgians from the past of Greece.

Thus I put him on the trail of William Van Moerbeke, a Flemish Dominican from Moerbeke who, until his death in 1286, was a bishop in the Western or Latin diocese of Corinth. That Catholic Diocese was founded after the Fourth Crusade, like the other Frankish interests that we described earlier. Van Moerbeke is still remembered today as a translator of Aristotle on behalf of his friend Thomas Aquinas. Others, such as American blogger and historian Diana Gilliland Wright, are intrigued by him, because he would have lived a double life as a diplomat and an intelligence agent.

I heard the story from Ambassador Van den Reeck, who in a previous life had already explored the flat landscape of Argolis and ended up in a village called Merbeka with the Church of the Dormition of the Virgin. The village where the spirit of Van Moerbeke still wanders is called Aghia Triada today, after the young independent country had nationalized all Turkish sounding names. The only fly in the ointment was the fact that Merbeka was not Turkish, but Flemish. For many, Merbeka refers indeed to Moerbeke. Maybe one day we can straighten this out, but what intrigues me, more than his life, is his death.

In the blog of Diana Gilliland Wright I read: 'Someone has written a dissertation on Moerbeke and the church, but this person will not allow it to be read "because someone might steal my ideas".

I have been told that this person claims Moerbeke built the Church of the Dormition of the Virgin as a burial chapel for himself. If there is actual evidence connecting the burial chamber with Moerbeke, the evidence has not been made available. We have no idea if or why Moerbeke thought he wanted to be buried in the Argolis.'

In an email Wright adds: 'I am quite sure that Moerbeke died in Italy. His will was written there, and people tended to write their wills when death was breathing heavily upon them.'

The hunger of this taphophile has awakened a new quest for another lost tomb – perhaps in Greece, perhaps in Italy?

Of course, I also put the young man on the track of Vesalius. The intention was to publish newsletters commenting on this quest for his grave, enriched by the young man's research. When I read his biographical sketch of Vesalius, I immediately recognized its most important resource, and I quote the link on the website: 'Brief Biography – follow here, as an introduction, a brief overview of Vesalius's life. For more information please contact the various bio-bibliographies.'

Instead of rewriting this episode a second or even a third time, I prefer the words of one of the most complete Vesalius bibliographers ever: Maurice Biesbrouck. I simply shortened somewhat his biographical sketch of the adult life of Andreas Vesalius.

'At the end of the same year (1537), we discover Vesalius at the University of Padua, then the most advanced medical faculty in Europe. According to the records he passed some exams on December 1 and 3 with brilliant results. Two days later, he obtained his doctorate in medicine, and, the very next day, he took over as successor to Paolo Colombo from Cremona, who was holding the chair of surgery. As a result he was also forced to teach anatomy. On December 6, he immediately began the dissection of an 18-year-old boy, who was taken from his grave by some of his students. After the dissection, Vesalius built his skeleton according to his new technique, which has remained almost unchanged until today. Unlike Sylvius in Paris, Vesalius took notes about any discrepancy between what he saw and what Galen had written. For the convenience of his students, and at their request, Vesalius drew three plates (…) based upon this dissection and asked Johan Stefan Kalkar, also a Fleming and pupil of Titian, to draw three skeletal figures. The six plates were issued as the Tabulae Anatomicae sex (six anatomical plates) by Vitalis Venetus (Venice, 1538). They constitute the first serious attempt to portray what was seen, but they still contain Galenic elements such as the five-lobed liver and a sternum of seven parts. As Vesalius, however, seemed to have more human bodies at his disposal, his initially reserved attitude changed abruptly: he didn't believe anything of Galen any more, until he could prove it himself. During that time he also gave several guest lectures, as in Bologna with professor Albius. (...)

In August of 1543, Vesalius (...) received the first copy of his masterpiece, *De Humani Corporis Fabrica Libri Septem*, Seven Books on the Construction of the Human Body. It was brilliantly edited in Basel by John Oporinus, professor of classical philology and friend of Vesalius. Haller (1708–1777), a physiologist from Bern, wrote about the *Fabrica* (...): "(it is) an immortal work, which makes all the earlier writings as good as redundant."

Shortly after the publication of his *Fabrica*, Vesalius, at his request, entered the service of Charles V as a regular family doctor or 'physician familiaris ordinary'. In the same period he married Anna van Hamme from Vilvoorde and in July 1545 they had a daughter, also named Anna, their only child. (...)

On the occasion of his abdication, on October 25, 1555, Emperor Charles V curtailed the employment of the bulk of his household staff as well as his personal physician. As a reward for his services, Vesalius, on April 21, 1556, received the title of Comes Palatinus or Count of the Holy Lateran Palace, one of the highest honors, to which various financial benefits were linked. He then joined Charles's son, Philip II, with whom he embarked on a ship on August 23, 1559 bound for Spain. In Madrid during the following years, he never felt really at home. There were no possibilities there to practise anatomy. At the end of 1561, he wrote to Gabriele Fallopio (1523–1562) in response to his anatomical work, *Observationes Anatomicae*, a letter that was so extensive that he turned it into a book, *Gabrieli Fallopii Observationum Exam* (Study of the [anatomical] observations of Gabriele Fallopio). It was the last of a total of ten works that he left behind.' Thus wrote Maurits Biesbrouck.

DE DVODECIM SVPERIORIS MAXIL

læ oßibus, in quorum classem naßi oßa etiam referuntur. Caput IX.

PRIMA NONI CAPITIS FIGVRA.

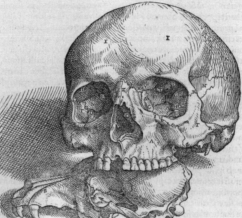

PRIMAE NONI CAPITIS FIGVRAE, EIVSDEM'QVE
characterum Index.

H AE C figura anteriorem caluariæ sedem exprimit, maxillæ superioris oßa, quàm datum est accuratißimè, ostensura. Humanæ autem caluariæ caninam subiecimus, ut Galeni superioris maxillæ oßium descriptio, leuiori negotio à quouis intelligatur. Præterea, ut oculorum sedes, ac in ijs apparentes suturæ oßaq́, quoad fieri licet, spectarentur, hominis caluariam occipitio inniti, & anteriori sede super caninam erigi oportuit. Præsentis autem figuræ characterum indicem ita digeram, ut maiusculi Græcorum, maxillæ superioris oßibus (quæ sex utrinq́, erunt) primùm adhibeantur: reliquis autem oßibus & suturis, ut sors fert, omnes accommodentur. Cæterùm priores aliquot characteres ostendendis foraminib. capitis iuuabunt, quare etiam illi ad Caput his dicandũ opportunè reseruabuntur. Sunt autẽ illi A, B, usque ad I.

I I *Frontis os. I etiam ponitur in oculorum sedibus, eam frontis oßis partem notans, quæ superiorem oculorum sedium regionem constituit.*

K *Verticis os sinistrum.*   L   *Sinistri temporis os.*

M *Mammillaris processus sinister, iuxta quem processus stylum referens etiam occurrit.*

N *Cuneiforme os, in sinistri temporis cauo & in dextri oculi sede N insignitur. In sinistri autem oculi sede G & H reponuntur, idem os indicantia: quanquam illi characteres huius sedis foraminibus ostendendis peculiariter subseruiant. Ad hæc, N quoq́ reponitur ad intimum sinistri lateris dentem, notans cuneiformis oßis particulam, & dein suturam id os à superiori maxilla hac in sede diuidentem.*

Γ Γ *Hoc os, nobis primum maxillæ superioris numerabitur. ac Γ in oculi sede positũ, huius oßis partem notat, in oculi sede conspicuã. Circumscribitur uerò id os præsentis figuræ a, b, Q, R & P, quos characteres suis locis sensim explicabo.*

Δ *In sinistri oculi sede Δ tantũ apparet, superioris maxillæ secundũ os indicans, quod terminatur sutura Δ & C literis proximè ac uelut orbiculatim ambiente, & quodãmodo etiã X, V, c.*

Θ *In sinistri quoque oculi sede Θ tantùm occurrit, tertium maxillæ superioris os indicans, quod V, T, c & d intercipitur.*

ΛΛ

Illus. 12: From the monumental Fabrica of Vesalius, v plate 29.

20. Vesalius and the holy grave

'I gladly complied with his devout request
and have allowed him to travel to Jerusalem
and visit the Holy Sepulchre Church of our Saviour.'

This is a key phrase from the letter of January 1564 which Philip II wrote to the Embassy of Spain in Venice asking if his doctor Andreas Vesalius could be supported, to enable him 'to get to Jerusalem safely so that he could return swiftly to his post and resume his work for me'. A few days after Vesalius's arrival in Venice, the Embassy replied: 'As soon as possible, he will be well equipped to sail to Cyprus and from there to Jerusalem. He says he'll hurry.'

Two weeks later, in late May, the Embassy reported that 'the troop transport for Cyprus and Corfu, with Vesalius on board, could not sail because of bad weather'. Even though the letter would not arrive on time, on May 29, 1564, the Nuncio and Protector of the Holy Places, wanted to thank and reassure Philip II 'for the royal gift of five hundred ducats that Dr. Vesalius, pious pilgrim, has brought as an aid to the shrines for the Catholic faithful in Jerusalem'.

These are quotes from four letters that were discovered by the Spanish historian José Baron Fernandez in 1962 and presented two years later at an international conference in Basel.

Recently the Flemish Vesalius specialists Omer Steeno and Maurice Biesbrouck reminded us once again about the existence of these letters in the journal of the *International Society for the History of Medicine*[2].

The rediscovered documents state in black and white that the doctor had left for Jerusalem out of devotion, with a royal gift in his luggage and that his employer eagerly awaited his return. This was a pilgrimage, a diplomatic mission, or both.

The myth that Vesalius was a victim of the inquisition is as difficult to erase from the mind as the idea that he died in a shipwreck.

In his book of 1953 Nicolas Barbianis gives us a beautiful account of the possible reasons why Vesalius left Spain. A Flemish student and Maurice Biesbrouck translated Barbianis's list of reasons, which I quote below:

'Vesalius could no longer stand his wife, nor the hatred and intrigues of the courtiers, nor tiring life at court and he had a dislike of fanatical priests. The pilgrimage was a vow after an illness, an expiation for dissecting people, or a death sentence given as punishment for an autopsy performed by Vesalius in which it was claimed the victim was still alive, a conviction that was later converted into a pilgrimage.'

These are the reasons given for his departure from Spain, which until today still live on. Ask anyone why Vesalius travelled to Jerusalem and this is the answer you would get.

There is, however, to this day, not a single piece of evidence that he was convicted and sentenced to death nor that this death sentence was converted into a pilgrimage nor that he fled from anything. On the contrary and again, as shown above, the letters of Philip II prove that it was a pilgrimage or a diplomatic mission, or both.

If Vesalius's biographers wish to keep this myth alive, despite the evidence to the contrary, I can only assume that this says more about them than about proper historical research.

The American philosopher Stephen Hicks, with whom I have exchanged a few emails regarding this issue, wrote an Internet article about Vesalius and philosophy, which I quote here:

'Suppose you're an early physician - your patients suffer and die, and you don't know why. One option is not to think much of it: bad stuff happens, people die, accept it. It takes an active mind - curiosity, interest, follow through - for science to get going. *Why* do people die? Even if you do decide to think about it, there are further obstacles.'

To name but a few obstacles, he lists: metaphysics, morality and aesthetics, and *epistemological* barriers, tradition. I can understand this reasoning. That not everybody jumps over hurdles in the same way, I can understand as well. Vesalius himself had to overcome many obstacles along the way. He was a wise man, and would not have made light of difficulties that he had to overcome; when he was robbing a grave for example or the first time that he put a scalpel into a human body and the smell of a corpse hit him in the face, or when he found that his teachers were wrong or when his peers accused him of taking things too far, and so on. The clash between Catholicism and Protestantism was very prominent at this time, but he kept himself aloof. He himself said so; I quote from the new translation of Karger's *New Fabrica* by Daniel Garrison and Malcolm H. Hast, on the website of Karger about *Transforming Vesalius 1514–2014.*

'To avoid running afoul of some "idle talker" here, or some critic of doctrine, I shall completely avoid this dispute concerning the types of soul and their location. For, today, you will find many judges of our most truthful and sacred religion, especially among the natives of my country, and if they heard anyone muttering about the opinions of Plato, Aristotle, Galen, or their interpretations about the soul, even when the subject is Anatomy (which these subjects are especially likely to be discussed), they leap to the conclusion that such a person is in doubt about the Faith or has some uncertainty about the immortality of Souls, without taking into consideration that physicians (provided they do not come rashly into their art or wish to apply inappropriate remedies to a sickened member) must think about the faculties that govern us, how many kinds there are, how each is marked, in what member of a living thing each is established, and besides these (if we can grasp it with the mind) chiefly what the substance and essence of the soul is.

It is as if no one could make a statement about the ideas of those august authors without impiety or the smallest lapse of faith, or even support their reasoning with other new arguments, or refute the trivial arguments of others. It is as if no discourse or inquiry were otherwise possible about the sacred faith by which we are saved, with the aid of pious good works and by which the souls of men gain a blessed eternity, except with reference to these latter dogmas and the opinions which a feeble human reason has supplied in this matter.'[3]

In this communication Vesalius clearly states his opinion that science does not affect faith. Whatever science may discover. To discover new things is the essence of Science. I read, in the text, no unequivocal statement about the faith of Vesalius. What I have read is that Vesalius accuses others who see his work as a statement of religious disbelief.

The translator of the above text, Daniel H. Garrison, puts it another way: 'Vesalius (...) allowed the soul to remain the exclusive preserve of religious zealots (about whom he had some choice words elsewhere)'.

The theorem of Garrison is in an article on the Karger website about the new translation, entitled 'The Long Arm of the Inquisition.' The summary subtitle reads: 'As bold and radical as Vesalius's scientific methods could be, his stance was more circumspect on matters of religion and the soul.' The illustration that accompanies the article is a print by Thomas Rowlandson (1756–1827) on the Spanish Inquisition.

Does Garrisson suggest with such a title, introduction and illustration that the anatomist might have got himself into trouble with the Inquisition? From the words of Vesalius, I can only conclude that he was very careful in front of his fanatical opponents, and was no doubt quite right in this. The tone of the article above is written from assumptions that were false: the conviction. Why does Garrison here use the lubricant of the Inquisition? To use the words of the Flemish writer Joris Tulkens.

I have already referred to his novel *Vesalius*.

In an e-mail Joris Tulkens wrote to me, he stated: 'This is not a biography, nor a historical study. It is a historical novel.' In another e-mail, in response to a comment by Omer Steeno about the lack of evidence of a conviction by the Inquisition, he adds: 'I have emphasized twice (introduction and cover) that I describe what might have happened, (...) hoping to highlight the genius of Vesalius and to demonstrate the importance of his refreshing approach to Science (no more deductive, but inductive). A conflict with the Inquisition is therefore the lubricant with which I am trying to achieve this.'

Historical confusion about the Inquisition as a lubricant for what? I fully realize that we are talking about literature here, but does not Tulkens drown his subject matter? Take the study of the soul that intersects all the storylines? The source material is certainly enjoyable literature, but has more to do with the dichotomy between liberalism and faith than with scientific innovation.

This way the fictionalized biography is turned into a committee report of some ethical issue more than it is a historical thriller, with the difference being that the contrast between good and evil has been left behind a long time ago.

On my Facebook page about Andreas Vesalius I have tried to show, by using the example of the prints from his *Fabrica*, that the humanist Vesalius avoided controversies of his time by emphasizing the ideals of antiquity.

In the centre of the frontispiece of the *Fabrica* the mask of a satyr gets all the attention. Some think that the mask refers to the Greek theatre. They conclude that Vesalius and his illustrator van Calcar wished to make it clear that anatomy should be taught and demonstrated, which indeed often happens in theatres as this print clearly shows. Others point out that this is not just a satyr. This is Marsyas who challenged Apollo to hold a musical competition. Marsyas lost, however, and Apollo punished him by skinning him alive. Marsyas appears throughout the *Fabrica*, but is not always recognizable.

One of the alterations made in the *Fabrica* of 1555 is a new large, illuminated letter V. In the letter V, there is an illuminated scene of Apollo flaying Marsyas. And all this takes place within the letter V of Vesalius!

Many want us to see the flayed Marsyas as the Holy Saint Bartholomew, just as Michelangelo depicted him in the Sistine Chapel with his own skin in his hand. This apostle died a martyr's death after he was skinned alive. Nevertheless Vesalius did not wish to use the symbolism of Saint Bartholomew, but he did want to use the victim of Apollo, that is, Marsyas.

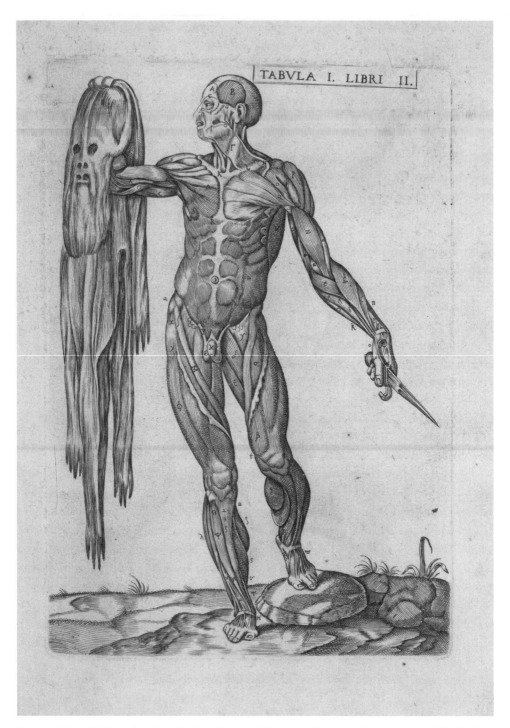

Illus. 13: From De Vivae Imagines Partium Corporis Humani, of Joannes Valverda, inspired by Vesalius.

Throughout the *Fabrica* Christian images and references can be seen from this angle. There is the supposed similarity between the autopsy by Vesalius on the title page of the *Fabrica* and 'The Lamentation over the Dead Christ' by the Italian painter Andrea Mantegna. One can recognize the anatomical details of the thorax, the stigmata, the genitals, and the drapes. Would Vesalius, after what we have seen above, have actually had the guts to replace Christ with a woman and her reproductive organs? The woman as material prima and the man at the centre of the universe, or should I say, the centre of the universe of Vesalius?

The dissecting scene on the title page of the *Fabrica* seems to illustrate a sacred ceremony or ritual, which is conducted by Vesalius. The symbolism is reinforced by the fictional audience, which appears to be a sample of people from his time. Between the three groups of spectators around Vesalius, who is depicted as a pioneer, Dominique Raichvarg, French Professor in the History of sciences, recognizes politicians such as the Mayor of Padua, artists and intellectuals such as the painter Titian, publishers like Oporinus and colleague anatomists, both pro and contra Galen. Even Luther, German Protestant reformer, is in the audience.

If Vesalius is not just the teacher in a classroom of anatomy and his guests are not just spectators or students, what is going on here? Are they perhaps a classic chorus that reacts to what Vesalius tells the reader? Or are they members of a jury of prominent people who evaluate Vesalius's work or lectures? Is the dissected one perhaps the holy book? Some researchers such as Andrew Cunningham interpret this image as Vesalius actually reading and dissecting the body. And hereby going so far, that they see this book/body as a response to the Lutheran question *Sola Scriptura*: read the script, only the script and not the commentaries and traditional commentaries of the Catholic Church that in this instance represent the Galen Followers.

Shall I call this stream of interpretations to a halt and quote Vesalius once again, from the preface of the *Fabrica* (in English translation)?

> 'Yet I surmise that out of the entire Apolline discipline of medicine, and indeed all natural philosophy, nothing could be produced more pleasing or welcome to your Majesty than research in which we recognize the body and the spirit, as well as a certain divinity that issues from a harmony of the two, and finally our own selves (which is the true study of mankind).'

In footnote 63, Garrison and Hast add: '... a sentiment combining the Apolline "know thyself" and Protagoras' "man is the measure of all things'.

To his patron and client Vesalius explains: 'Because it is inevitable that you would only be interested in the science of the universe, you will be introduced to the construction of the most perfect of all creatures. You will be pleasantly surprised to read about the place and the instrument of the immortal soul: a home that is amazingly similar to the universe, and that the classics appropriately named the microcosm.'

In the text, he often calls the constructor of the human body, the Creator. Is Vesalius a creationist? If he says that the beauty of man reflects the beauty of its architect, then does that makes him a supporter of 'the intelligent design'? Why did he call upon Him so often? Sometimes, even as The Great Architect of the Universe? Was he perhaps a pre-Freemason? A Neo-platonist? Very often he describes Him as Nature? Was he a Darwinist *avant la lettre*?

The genius of Vesalius is so great that he is recuperated by all denominations. For some, his reaction 'against' prevails, for others his innovativeness prevails. It is easy to place his scientific achievements in history; even in the light of what these achievements mean today, his genius can carry a political or religious meaning.

If biographers talk about the Inquisition, they express their own point of view, their own religious beliefs. For me it is clear: Vesalius can be honoured by 'free-thinking' theologists, 'non-dogmatic' atheists and anybody in between.

Vesalius has been dead for four hundred and fifty years, but his genius lives on. If we find his bones we will certainly not find the bone, which was believed in his time, to be able to reconstruct his body on the Day of the Judgement. The Arabian occult and obscure philosophers called this bone Albadaran. 'It is better known by the superstitious than by students of anatomy,' Vesalius said.

When I visited the Holy Sepulchre of Jerusalem two things impressed me a great deal: one was the great variety of faiths that can co-exist within the one church, and the other was the Stone of Anointment or Unction. This limestone slab was placed just past the impressive wooden entrance gate during the renovation of 1808–1810 to replace a 12th century slab. If this earlier slab or a similar plate had laid there in 1564, Vesalius would have had a reflective moment. Such a slab was used to wash and embalm and oil a cadaver, which was then wrapped in a shroud. No doubt Vesalius would have been brought to silence as, like me, he reflected on the function of the slab; who knows, he might have even found them useful for his dissections.

So thoughts were released about what the stone slab represented: several churches have hung their own type of lamps above the marble bed to remind each and everyone about the importance it holds. The surrounding areas of the Basilica were established in memory of a character who, for two thousand years, affected people in one way or another.

How ironic is the fact that the tomb, given to the minister by a rich man who had prepared it for himself, eventually ended up empty? Here arose another thought when I saw that picture of a skeleton kneeling; inspired by the thinking skeletons of Vesalius, I was reminded that William Cheselden (in *Osteographia* or the *Anatomy of the Bones*, London, 1733) chose this position to place 'the character in a broader context'.

21. An inquisition for all seasons

For this I read the meaning of this end:
There are two ways of spreading light; to be
The candle or the mirror that reflects it.
I let my wick burn out – there yet remains
To spread an answering surface to the flame
That others kindle.

From 'Vesalius in Zante (1564)' by Edith Wharton

The three Vesalius Momenti, held respectively in Athens, Zakynthos and Leuven, had been very constructive meetings. Friends of Vesalius, as I had begun to call them, from Greece, Belgium and the United Kingdom, worked together in an ad hoc organizing committee towards the forthcoming Vesalius Continuum celebration on Zakynthos. Instead of dividing the committee into subcommittees and assigning functions, we chose the natural way of working. We hoped that personal interests would take the upper hand over personal agendas. Pascale Pollier is the cement that holds everyone together; the exhibition and the monument are her special projects. As coordinator in Greece, I tried to guide the search for the grave away from a romantic quest into a professional research quest.

During that summer of 2012, this quest had become as fertile as it was realistic. Spurred on by Cerberus and Pavlos Plessas, the attention had shifted from Kalogerata to Santa Maria delle Grazie. At the same time I made a big effort to defuse the smear campaign of the lost monument on Kalogerata, whilst nevertheless safeguarding the heritage of Nicolas Barbianis. According to the final report of the meeting in Leuven, the search for the grave, from now on, had to be officially carried out by the authorities.

Yet the darkest pages of this story would be written in the weeks and months following the Leuven meeting. As some could only view the tension between reason and faith through the prism of their own beliefs, all kinds of forces were released during this period, sadly not always with the promotion of Vesalius as the ultimate goal.

To recap: the original seekers had learned, from the Dutch archaeologist Gert Jan van Wijngaarden, who the current owner of the hill on Kalogerata was. The construction on the sharp bend in Andre Vesal Street towards the village Pantokratoras was thought to become a diving school. With the excuse that they were looking for a Dutch diving instructor, they had spoken to the current owner and founder. He knew of no gravestone and sent them away from his magic mountain. That was in the winter of 2011.

The morning after the second Momentum in Zacantha Hotel, in July 2012, Constantinos (Kostas) Geladas, the President of the City Council Pantokratoras, picked up Pavlos Plessas and myself, with his red Susuki, so that we could explore the Hill of Kalogerata together. I left my car in a side street of the famous 'strip of Laganas'.

On the way back Geladas received a call from the previous owner of the land, who was accused by everyone of the disappearance of the Vesalius monument. We asked if we could meet him.

On the strip of Laganas, Geladas gave some quick instructions to the workers who were cleaning up from the previous night of party-goers. In the American-inspired coffee shop/cocktail bar, on the western side of the strip, we were the first guests. Black blinds kept the bright sun at bay. Between the giant television screens and hubcaps on the wall and the shadows of cleaning ladies, we ordered our first espresso of the day.

The giant character with the shaved head insisted on speaking exclusively in Greek. Of the discourse regarding the stolen stone there remains, until today, only negative echoes: against the English language, against all politicians, against anyone who accuses his family. He knows nothing about the stone, as he claims he was abroad when the stone disappeared.

We gave him the message that we were not behind the police investigation. If we ever found out what exactly happened to the stone, we would convince the others to drop the complaint. Sadly that seed would not germinate.

On November 2, 2012 the following article appears in the local press: 'The President of the Medical Association has commented on the research that the Prosecutor has ordered to find the Vesalius monument: the local authorities should have restored this monument a long time ago, long before the Department of Justice got interested'.

The paper reiterates that the Laganas police have convoked the President of the City Council and the owners of the site. Pavlos Kapsambelis says that the case has been brought by the Medical Association, in collaboration with a group of concerned citizens.

'The culprits are known, but everyone is silent. Memory loss is unacceptable, hence this complaint. The loss of that monument is damaging to our reputation.'

At the Second Momentum on Zakynthos Kostas Geladas and Pavlos Kapsambelis were still socialising together.

On that occasion I had invited our compatriot William Nagels. I knew from Omer Steeno that the Belgian businessman was a developer of construction projects on Zakynthos. When I had sent him a Vesalius brochure he had not responded. That he was still interested, I heard through the whispering winds of the sailing doctors. Their mail was not addressed to me: 'We know there will be a reception on Zakynthos for the "Friends of Vesalius" in July on Zakynthos; we have a friend who has a large house and spends a great deal of time there. He has many contacts with local authorities on Zakynthos. He also wants to help to shape the Vesalius project. He will attend the reception. If he should be needed in any way, or if you need to discuss anything with him, you can let us know and we will pass on the message to him.'

The acquaintance with William and his wife was pleasant. In his enthusiasm, I think I might have recognized symptoms of the Vesalius Bug that ultimately infects everyone.

In November, the proposal of collaboration becomes concrete. The businessman announces a trip to Zakynthos and asks about a photo of the missing memorial stone of Kalogerata and if there is any interest in replacing the stone. 'I've already spoken to a number of people and I think it is no problem to collect the necessary funds.' The sailing recipient of the email responds in an inimitably enthusiastic style.

In the weeks that follow, William Nagels gets a whole network going. Architects and their associations, journalists and politicians again go further to investigate the missing stone. The case is re-examined and private collections are investigated, but the search has revealed nothing. The stone is not valuable enough and was probably used in the construction of a house, as was the common practice throughout this entire history.

I myself have always been convinced that, instead of looking for the missing stone, funds and energy would be better spent in searching for the lost tomb. After some bilateral consultations, Pollier responded on November 12 with admirable diplomacy, in a correspondence to her old and new friends: 'I think it's a noble idea to remake the stone, certainly. I think that Nikos Barbianis would be very happy that his grandfather is honoured in this way. I also would like to let you know that there are already plans to make a sculpture, a new memorial of an écorché or a flayed man (based on one of the images in the *Fabrica*), but there is certainly room to think about a possible collaboration.'

The fact that the stone was the subject of a judicial inquiry was another reason to give this up. Unfortunately not everyone was convinced. On Wednesday, December 12, 2012 an article appeared in the *Ermis* newspaper by Kostas Geladas, Chairman of the Council of Pantokratores, announcing that a new monument for Vesalius will be created. It will replace the old one, but not at the same place; it will be located a street further away. A Belgian architect will provide technical assistance, so says the article.

Much later, on Monday, April 15, 2013 I was approached by the same lobby group. 'At the place where Vesalius was shipwrecked, we want to establish a new monument. The design is finished. The building material is white Zakynthian stone used by local builders. Everything is ready. I'm just waiting on your arrival to Zakynthos to give you all the information you require.'

A week later, I spoke with the lobbyist at the Phoenix Hotel. On a paper serviette he drew me the design of a rectangular shrubbery marked with four poles with a chain attaching them and a large flat tombstone. 'The tomb of Vesalius,' he said proudly. Casually he tried to convince the Vesalius Conference team to move the venue to a five-star hotel on the other side of the island to the city's theatre. Why? 'Because the theatre will never be ready in time.' I left as I also had a meeting with Vice Mayor Akis Ladikos. They crossed each other in the spacious entrance door without a greeting.

> 'People of Zakynthos are so immersed in local politics, their political beliefs are so deep that they even fear on their deathbed that a priest from another party would be administering poison instead of the last sacraments.'

Thus wrote the American author Edith Wharton when she sailed to the island in 1888 with her sailing ship Vanadis; she was only 26 when she wrote her first travel story, that was rediscovered in 1991 in a French library.

22. Vesalius Momentum IV: Antwerp

On May 2, 2014 at 5:15 a.m., Zakynthos was moved with a magnitude of 3.3. That is very weak: I do not think that the earthquake even woke up the locals. I was already awake, as if I was waiting for it.

The days that had preceded this had also been moving. I had a meeting on the island with Maria Leventi and Eleni Andrianakou, representatives of Ibis El Greco, a conference organizer with offices in Crete and Corfu. The owner of this agency is Yves Maebe, Honorary Consul of Belgium in Crete. Together we wanted to consolidate a few aspects of the conference. A week earlier, in the middle of the election campaign, the newspapers had announced that the promised venue for our conference, the new theatre of the town, could not be finished in time. The necessary funds could not be released in time. I had been tipped off a few weeks earlier. The opposition was also aware, as the President of the Medical Association stated in the newspaper, that he had withdrawn from the conference, for many more reasons than only this.

Meanwhile, the lobbying of Laganas to become host to the conference had increased. On April 25, 2014, the Associations of Hotel and Room Owners requested, in the newspaper, that the monument and the conference to be moved to Laganas. They announced that they would like to discuss this with us.

To untie that knot, on April 29, 2014, I brought together a network of people at the Red Rock Café. The name of the establishment refers to a book by local author Gregory Xenopoulos. As far as I can tell from the summary, it is a local version of *Wuthering Heights*, the 1847 rending love story of Emily Brontë. At Red Rock Café, and in a separate meeting the next day, the folds of the Greek love story were not ironed out either. We were prepared and willing to support one of their activities but Laganas wanted to continue and honour the story that Vesalius was shipwrecked on the deserted beach. During the last day of my official visit, on May 2, two competing local newspapers covered the story, stating that an agreement had been reached but that the decision would be announced at a press conference after the elections. Whilst announcing the political earthquake that would follow soon, the earth trembled slightly that day.

Battling against this force of nature, a sailing boat arrived on that very same day in Zakynthos. On board: Ann Van de Velde, Marc De Roeck and friends.

No doubt, down to professional and practical conditions, the ensemble missed the above mentioned meetings. I, however, had planned an alternative programme with a visit of the Vesalius painting by Mrs Eleni Gounari in the First Lyceum, and a guided tour to the Santa Maria delle Grazie area, by Pavlos Plessas and I.

Illus. 14:
In a landscape with ruins, the muscle man, on plate 98, inspiration for the monument of Pascale Pollier and Richard Neave.

The sailing club and the De Roeck entourage have, without question, worked hard towards the financing of the new monument of Pascale Pollier and Richard Neave in Zakynthos and the sponsoring of the Vesalius Momentum in Antwerp. I attended one of their meetings in the house of one of their members. The strategy that they mapped out to finance the large new monument, by pre-selling a dozen facial reconstruction portraits in bronze, holds strong to this day. The decision to sculpt the plinth in Zakynthos, which was made possible by the hospitality and practical support of William Nagels, was also made during that very meeting. Meanwhile, Nagels generously provided Pollier with a large, white Zakynthian stone.

The unveiling of the original facial reconstruction portrait, which was made in cement, has finally taken place, in the regional hospital of Hasselt, Limburg, where one of the sponsors works. The statue was unveiled by Omer Steeno.

The bust, cast in bronze by Foundry De Clercq-Ginsberg, was unveiled during the Fourth Momentum in Antwerp. The event on November 23, 2013 was sponsored and organised by BIOMAB.

As with previous editions of Vesalius Momenta BIOMAB too had an eye for a certain symbolism. The accommodation was booked in Elzenveld, today a modern hotel and seminar centre. In the thirteenth century, however, the first *hospitale infirmorum* [where the sick are taken care of] of Antwerp moved to this complex. Where could we better honour Andreas Vesalius than in the compound of a former hospital, in which the hospital halls, the convent and chapel, erected around 1400, are still tangible? The actual meeting took place in the Greek House in Antwerp.

In the early evening the Flemish television channel, One, recorded an interview with Pascale Pollier, in the studio of the sculptor Chantal Pollier, who sculpted the plinth and the coat of arms of the monument. This brief interview was broadcast in the afternoon and evening news.

'They were all there, the éminences grises of the Vesalius scholars. Professors Omer Steeno, Maurice Biesbrouck and Robert Van Hee, Pavlos Plessas, paediatrician Mark Gardiner from University College London, pathologist and anatomist and writer Johan Van Robays, the Belgian consul in Greece, Theo Dirix, and the Greek Ambassador Constantin Chalastanis who had the honour of officially unveiling the Vesalius bronze,' thus Henk van Nieuwenhove opened his article in Belgian medical newspaper *Artsenkrant* on Friday, November 29, 2013. 'The Ambassador of Greece,' he writes, 'showed himself to be particularly happy, in his inaugural speech, with the interest shown in the Belgian scientist Vesalius and the impact that he has had on the Greek island. He concluded his speech with: "Vesalius lives, Zakynthos lives".'

23. Not just an epitaph

The Russian diplomat/civil servant, philhellene and poet, Count Peter Ivanovitch Kapnist (1830–1898), grandson of the more famous Vasili Kapnist, wanted to be buried on Zakynthos. As he chanted in one of his verses, preferably towards the sea, where he would be eternally cradled asleep by the sound of rolling waves.

After his death on August 18, 1897, his bones were transferred to a grove above the coast in Xirokestallo, between Argasi and Vasilikos, in the south-eastern tail of the island. There he lies today, right behind a house on the edge of a farm with pigs, turkeys and chickens. He looks over the sea to the mainland and the crusader castle at Kilini.

Under the monumental white marble cross with graffiti under the crossbar, lies a fresh egg. The crypt in bricks, half buried under the ground, is sealed with a white marble plate. The bottom right corner has been broken in an attempt to break open the mausoleum. On the plate is the presentation of an eternally burning oil lamp.

Above his name, in Russian and translated into Greek, are a few verses carved in the weathered, veined marble stone. These verses have been obscured in the photographs that I took and have also faded in my memory. The essence of these verses however, that life is a ladder to eternity, resonates in my head.

Zakynthos's dead poets and their graves: Inexhaustible. Again it was Maria Sidirokastriti who showed Pavlos Plessas and me the way to this lost tomb. Yet, I suspect Plessas in reality is not very fond of this kind of epitaph and this kind of quest: too romantic. It is another kind of epitaph that gets him excited. As he shows in his reaction to this e-mail of Maurice Biesbrouck of August 14, 2012:

> 'In my re-issue of (...) Portraits *of Some Ancient and Recent Physicians and Philosophers* by Johannes Sambucus (1531–1584) of the edition of 1603, I found that Vesalius was buried in "D. [OMUS] Mariae", also according to him! He confirms the text of Vesalius's epitaph with the wrong age. He does not mention his source (F. N4v). The first edition of this work dates from 1574 (Antwerp: Plantin), ten years after Vesalius's death. Sambucus also knew that Vesalius was 50 years old when he died (F. A4V). So, this is additional evidence that V. was buried in the Santa Maria della Grazie, that the text of the epitaph itself was wrong, and the error not being made while transcribing it. This adds to the credibility of the other reports.'

Plessas, who behaves generally as a phlegmatic Briton, responds in a charmingly Greek manner:

'This is great news! Bravo! This is the 4th transcription of the epitaph, or are there more?

All slightly different yet basically the same. And this not counting the references by Schwallart and Pigafetta. Could this one be a contribution by Francis Raphelengius or his son as it is and not posthumous as mentioned in the first edition of 1574? Not that it matters, as Von Haimentorff's book was not published until 1621. For comparison I attach Von Haimentorff's version and the two by Archduke Salvator that O'Malley mentions (bottom of the page, after the epitaph of an important Frenchman who was buried inside the church).'

Not merely to understand this correspondence fully, I asked Pavlos Plessas to summarize and list all the evidence that points to the Santa Maria delle Grazie. His contribution below is copied entirely from our project proposal, addressed to pharmaceutical companies in the hope that they would sponsor our research:

- 'Christoph Fürer von Haimendorff [4] mentions Vesalius's grave in a coenobium called Mariae de Gratia in Zakynthos with the inscription '*ANDREAE VESALII BRUXELLENSIS TUMULUS, QUI OBIIT ANNO DOMINI M. D. LXIV. ID. OCTOBRIS, CUMEX HIEROSOLYMA REDIISSET, Anno Aetatis suae LVIII*' [Tomb of Andreas Vesalius from Brussels who died October 15, 1964, upon his return from Jerusalem, at the age of fifty eight]. Von Haimendorff's entry is dated August 4, 1565, when sailing past Corfu. The next entry, regarding the Strophades islands, is dated August 9. As the Strophades are only 30 miles approximately south of Zakynthos it seems that he stayed on the island for two or three days. As there was no question of quarantine for a ship coming from Venice he had ample time to visit the site. His journey was made less than a year after Vesalius's death and it is very unlikely he could have obtained the text of the inscription by means other than personal observation. The inscription's date of death is generally accepted as accurate and fully compatible with other evidence. Vesalius's age at the time of death is wrong, but this is easily explainable and does not raise any credibility issues.
- Giovanni Zuallardo (Johannes Schwallart or Zuallart) [5] gave a quite detailed description of Zakynthos in 1586, including some original material, such as the slave trade. This is corroborated by the writings of Pedro Teixeira two decades later, making it certain that Zuallardo visited the island. He mentions the tomb of Vesalius in a small Franciscan monastery called l'Annuntiata, where,

as he says, the Catholics buried their own dead and travellers. Annuntiata is another name by which Santa Maria delle Grazie was known. He mentions the inscription, clarifying it was no longer there as it had been taken by the Turks when they looted the island in 1571. The looting of the port area in 1571 is a well-known historical fact. Zuallardo is known amongst historians as a reliable source.

- Filippo Pigafetta may have visited Zakynthos more than once. He was certainly there in July 1586[6], at about the same time as Zuallardo, on his way to Syria and Palestine. He had, however, previously sailed to the eastern Mediterranean in 1568, 1571 and 1577. He cooperated with the Dutch mapmaker Abraham Ortelius and in the text of the Italian edition of his *Theatrum*[7] he added the following[8]:

"I, Filippo Pigafetta, add, leaving aside the dispute about the burial inscriptions of Cicero, who did not die on this island, that I have seen the grave of Andreas Vesalius of Brussels, famous anatomist, and the first one in our times, who knew with true Latin words and figures to illustrate the workings of the human body, as can be seen in his admirable books. Returning from a pilgrimage to the Holy Land, he finished his life here, after years of glory. A sign to his memory was fixed above the door of the Church of St Francis in gold letters on black velvet; which was later taken by the Turks in 1571; so, this island has been equally enobled with the bones of a person of such great fame."

Cicero was believed by many to have been buried in Santa Maria delle Grazie but Pigafetta obviously did not think so. The relevant burial inscription had been taken to Venice, probably before the death of Vesalius, so he would not have seen it. The Church of St Francis was inside the castle, and is described by Zuallardo. The Turks had besieged the castle in 1571 but not taken it and, hence, could not have looted the sign. Pigafetta, a man who had travelled extensively and seen many sights, must have, in the years that had passed, forgotten the name of the church and, remembering only that it belonged to the order of St Francis, confused the two churches' names. He also differs from Zuallardo because he speaks of a sign above the entrance and not an epitaph. This leaves open the possibility that the Turks removed not one but two Vesalius-related inscriptions. Pigafetta's testimony clearly does not carry the gravity of the other two but it undoubtedly supports them, albeit in its own confused manner.

On a side note, the Roman era grave with the name of Cicero is an indication that the site of Santa Maria delle Grazie may have been used as a burial ground since classical antiquity. In any case, there is reliable evidence that other men of importance were interned there after Vesalius, the best known being the author

Pierre Augustin Guys in the 19th century. Also, during building work at the site, two inscribed stone fragments of funerary monuments were unearthed, along with two non-inscribed marble panels. As you can see in the photographs below[9], one of the fragments bears the name BEVILAQVA. This surname is unknown in Zakynthos; however, according to the Zakynthos historian Spyridon De Biasi[10], a man named Devilaqua was given the position of public physician in the year 1593, just 29 years after the death of Vesalius.'
(Pavlos Plessas on April 26, 2013)

Now that Pavlos Plessas, Omer Steeno, Maurice Biesbrouck and Theodoor Goddeeris have dispelled all doubts about the presence of the tomb of Vesalius in or next to the Church of Santa Maria delle Grazie, the crucial question is: where exactly is the church and the graveyard?

As previously mentioned, on April 22 and 23, 2013, I organized a reconnaissance mission to ensure that the archaeologists Jan Driessen and Apostolos Sarris could assess whether such a strategy of determining its location, non-destructive checking of the data and eventually a dig would be attainable.

Illus. 15: a photograph of the Santa Maria delle Grazie, before the earthquake of 1953.

IN SEARCH OF ANDREAS VESALIUS

Their attention went to four districts (from east to west). About 100 metres east of the search for the Santa Maria Church is the Church of Aikaterini Ton Gripon. Although the earthquake of 1953 flattened the entire district, the area still retains parts of its original architecture and even the level of the street, with the old drainage still visual. Unlike the lower part of the city, the height level difference between the Renaissance and today is not too big.

In addition, we also paid attention to a well, dating from the Renaissance and an open and concreted square in Chioti Street. There is also a garden in Kolokotroni Street that is interesting for a more thorough investigation because it is accessible. It is about 10 metres west of the corner of Kolyva and about 15 metres west of the suspected site of the Santa Maria church.

And then, there is of course the parking area of the Palatino Hotel on Kolyva Street, about 15 metres south of the corner of that street and Kolokotroni Street. This plot, which during our visit measured a maximum of 10 metres wide to 15 deep, has meanwhile been reduced a bit. At the eastern edge of the parking, traces can be seen of a building that dates from after the earthquake and that was demolished to make a parking space about five years ago. Under the floor of 1953, against the eastern wall, some remnants of Renaissance masonry are visible that exhibit an arc. This suggests that it was originally part of a larger structure, about 20 metres south of where perhaps the Santa Maria Church was located.

We also visited the various museums of Zakynthos, which exhibit, among other artefacts, the scale model of Zakynthos and the photos of the Santa Maria delle Grazie Church in the Byzantine Museum, which helped us determine the physical reference points still visible today and to pinpoint them on the historical maps.

The project proposal has been sent to a few pharmaceutical companies. It was severely testing my patience but the next step in the quest finally arrived on Friday, February 14, 2014. It won't surprise anyone that it is Agfa HealthCare, world leader in the development of integrated IT systems for imagery in the health sector, that found a connection with a physician who, five hundred years ago, revolutionized science and medicine with illustrations of anatomy.

The digital map is being developed by the Institute for Mediterranean Studies (IMS) which has its office in Crete in Rethymnon. IMS is one of the research units of the Foundation for Research and Technology Hellas (FORTH). With the most advanced technologies in the field of Geophysical-Satellite Remote Sensing (GIS), the IMS is the only unit of FORTH active in human sciences, more specifically in an archaeological context.

In a second phase a geophysical approach should follow, as urban archaeological research should examine the place determined by the GIS. Only a Ground Penetrating Radar (GPR) and Electrical Resistivity Tomography (ERT) method can be applied there. But digging for the future will cost a lot of money.

24. From tombstone tourist to knight, genre Don Q

If Vesalius was alive today
he'd be scrutinizing his corpse in its grave
extracting DNA (DoNotAlter)

From 'Vesalius' by Bryan W. Green

'If you only plan one single reference to the anatomist in this Vesalius Year, you may want to refer to the region of Limburg where both Jan Driessen and I stem from,' I wrote on Wednesday March 26, 2014 with a wink to the largest regional sister newspapers of Belgium, *Het Belang van Limburg* and *de Gazet van Antwerpen*. A few hours later a journalist phoned Athens for more explanations, illustrations and a contact number for Jan Driessen and Pascale Pollier.

Even before the article hits the newspaper stand on Thursday, Vesalius Google Alerts are cramming my inbox. Almost all online newspapers in Flanders and Wallonia quoted from the article, distributed by the Belga news agency, the catchy phrase that Belgian archaeologists are looking for the tomb of Vesalius below a dusty parking lot on a Greek island.

I tell this press hounds story only to show that today only stories are picked up 'which are simple with clearly defined situations and recognizable personalities, (even though) reality (...) is much more nuanced and complex. But that is not very commercial, is it? Moreover, the preparatory work is often thankless and unpopular because it results in grey, obscure truths. Only a few researchers or historians score and then not always the hard working...'

This is in response to my frustration that no newspaper had quoted the names of my researchers – even though I had made it clear to the reporters that the clichés that I'm trying to disarm have been documented for years now by the infernal trio that plays a major role in this story. All credit goes to the Cerberus of the Vesalius Research in and around Belgium: Omer Steeno, Maurice Biesbrouck and Theodoor Goddeeris. They keep on tirelessly and passionately researching, repeating facts, tightening and confirming with other sources. Their articles appear in the magazine for members of the Alumni of the Medical Faculty of the University of Leuven and in prestigious international journals, including the *Vesalius, the journal of ISHM*.

Thanks to them alone the romantic quest of biomedical artists and a tombstone tourist with a diplomatic passport has found its place in a scientific framework. They have accepted that we make full use of this momentum to determine a new reference point. Whoever may be looking for the tomb of Andreas Vesalius from now on will know what the situation is on the ground today.

Let be be clear, however, I am not saying that we are giving up the search ourselves, in the meantime.

Following the press release, we were contacted by Dr. Martin Larmuseau, Laboratory of Forensic Genetics and Molecular Archaeology of the University of Leuven. Again, Omer Steeno was the messenger.

'The Laboratory of Forensic Genetics and Molecular Archaeology at the KU Leuven (headed by Prof. Ronny Decorte) specializes in genetic identification of ancient DNA. Known examples are: investigation into the true story of Louis XVII during the French Revolution, and the mummified head and blood that were wrongly attributed to the French king Henry IV and Louis XVI respectively (…).

If a grave (or more graves) were to be discovered during the search for the tomb of Vesalius, a genetic identification will indeed be necessary. This is possible through genetic genealogical approach where the mitochondrial DNA and/or Y-chromosomal variation is compared to (living) relatives in the direct maternal or paternal line. On the basis of the genealogical research of Jan Caluwaert this relationship would have already been found in direct maternal line, and it is therefore also possible to achieve a genetic identification, via the mitochondrial DNA.'

25. Taphophiles unite: a Geographical Information System (GIS), by Sylviane Déderix and Pavlos Plessas[II]

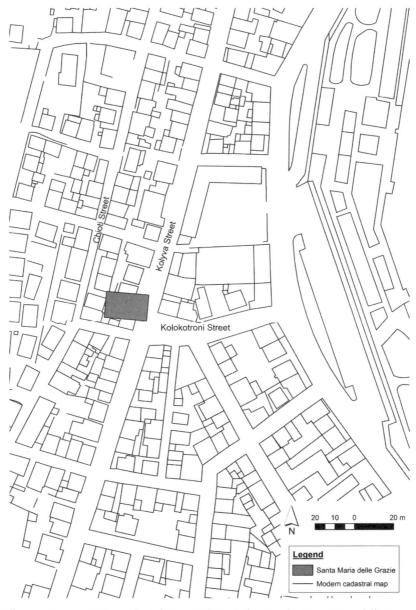

Illus. 16: Figure 3, GIS map by Sylviane Déderix, indicating the Santa Maria delle Grazie to the northwest of the crossroad of the current Kolyva and Kolokotroni streets.

As argued throughout this book, recent re-examinations of historical sources[12] have cast doubt on the long prevailing view that Vesalius died when his ship was wrecked near the shore of the island. Instead, it is more likely that he breathed his last breath before the gate of the town of Zakynthos, shortly after anchoring in the harbour. In the same vein, it is now reaffirmed that the anatomist's body was not buried on Laganas Beach but in town, in the courtyard of the church of Santa Maria delle Grazie.[13]

The church of Santa Maria delle Grazie may have been first founded in 1488.[14] In the early 16th century it was given to a newly established Franciscan brotherhood, together with parcels of land where a monastery was constructed.[15] The area was also used for a while for the burial of Catholics and foreigners.[16] The monastery was already in ruins in the first half of the 20th century, but the church continued to exist until 1953. That year, the Ionian Islands underwent a series of earthquakes. The tremors reached their height on August 12, when a magnitude 7.2 earthquake struck the region and caused the collapse of most of the buildings that were still standing in the town of Zakynthos. The fire that followed completed the destruction of the town, which was for the most part levelled to the ground. Zakynthos was then rebuilt according to a very different planning that did not involve the reconstruction of Santa Maria delle Grazie. Not only was the church buried under the new town, but its very location was also forgotten.

Material remains[17], local informants and ancient cartographic data[18] point globally in a similar direction: they suggest that the church of Santa Maria delle Grazie and the adjacent Franciscan monastery were located around the corner of the current Kolokotroni and Kolyva streets, in the north sector of the town. In order to assess the validity of this hypothesis and get a better understanding of the area prior to the ravaging earthquake and fire, it was decided to examine the historical maps of Zakynthos by making use of Geographical Information Systems (GIS).

GIS are computer-based tools for 'collecting, managing, integrating, visualizing, and analyzing geographically referenced information'[19] Relying upon centuries of cartography and more recent progress in computer sciences, GIS technology was first developed in the sixties to address geographical problems related to the management of natural resources, before being adopted and adapted within a wide range of disciplines.[20] Since human activity is spatial in nature, the technology soon sparked the archaeologists' and historians' interest.[21] As such, GIS have for instance been used to predict archaeological site location, support the protection of cultural heritage, or explore patterns of visibility, movement and territoriality in archaeological landscape contexts.[22] Within the framework of the quest for Vesalius's lost grave, GIS were implemented with the aim of overlaying modern and historical maps. The procedure, named *georeferencing* or *rectification*, consists of registering the individual maps in a geographic space so as to define their position in the real world by means of a known coordinate system[23] – in our case the Greek Geodetic Reference System of 1987 (EGSA '87).

The success of the procedure depends of course on the accuracy of the maps to be georeferenced. If a slight and consistent deviation is observed, it can be corrected to some extent by the transformation algorithms used by the GIS software. But in case of important and unpredictable inaccuracies, the result cannot be satisfactory. This issue is of crucial importance when dealing with historical maps that were produced before the development of modern cartographic technologies.

In our case, the map of interest was drawn in 1892 and published in 1970 by Dionysis Zivas, who pinpointed the location of significant buildings, among which is the church of Santa Maria delle Grazie.[24] However, since the coastline and the town plan changed drastically after the earthquake of 1953, it was not possible to overlay the particular map directly onto modern cartographic data. Intermediary steps were necessary. The methodology consisted therefore of travelling back in time and georeferencing maps from the most recent to the oldest. First of all, a modern cadastral map was rectified by means of geographic coordinates withdrawn from the satellite images of Google Earth. The result was extremely satisfactory as the particular map could be registered with minimal errors – total RMS error of 0.67 m when using a first order polynomial transformation algorithm.

The second step relied on a map that was stored in the personal archives of Yiannis Papadatos, a Zakynthian lawyer and the president of the Museum of D. Solomos and Eminent People of Zakynthos. The particular map predates the earthquake of 1953, although it was updated in 1954, before the reconstruction of Zakynthos. Even if the planning of the post-earthquake town bears little resemblance with its pre-earthquake predecessor, it was possible to register Yiannis Papadatos's map thanks to a Cartesian grid related to an old coordinate system (the so-called Hatt system) that was also referenced on the modern cadastral map. The determination of some ground control points associated with a few buildings that survived the earthquake, such as the church of Kyria ton Angelon, together with the use of a third polynomial transformation algorithm allowed to correct some imprecisions so that Papadatos's map could be registered with a sufficient degree of accuracy. Figure 1 illustrates the result of the rectification of both maps. It testifies to the extent of the alteration of the town after 1953. The changes are particularly striking in the southern half of the map, where the church and the monastery of Santa Maria delle Grazie are believed to be located, as even the road network follows a very different trajectory.

Eventually, the map of 1892 could be overlaid quite easily on Papadatos's map. This ancient map suffers from measurement imprecisions that could nevertheless be corrected by using the spline transformation algorithm. As illustrated in Figure 2, little changes occurred in the general layout of the northern part of Zakynthos between the last years of the 19th century and the mid-20th century. Only the coastline underwent significant modifications.

The GIS-based analyses of this set of modern and historical maps allows us to confirm the hypothesis that the ruins of Santa Maria delle Grazie are to be found to the northwest of the crossroad of the current Kolyva and Kolokotroni streets (see Figure 3). The road that ran in front of the church in the late 19th and early 20th century followed a different orientation than Koylva Street, with the consequence that Santa Maria delle Grazie is expected to lie partly below the street and partly below private properties. The question remains as to whether the late 19th century church of Santa Maria delle Grazie was located at the exact same spot as its 15th century predecessor. If so, the mortal remains of Vesalius might still lie around the Kolyva-Kolokotroni crossroad.

IN SEARCH OF ANDREAS VESALIUS

Conclusion: to be continued...

Can you imagine a diplomat being attracted more by an atlas of organs than by an atlas of maps, be it of the 16th or 21st century?

I have, however, always transported a copy of the 1589 European map of Gerardus Mercator to the offices in every country that I have served in. The map was even the frontispiece of the Vesalius brochure and was also exhibited during the first Momentum in Athens. The digitized GIS that Sylviane Déderix created from the neighbourhood of the Santa Maria delle Grazie in Zakynthos is the pinnacle of three years of intensive Vesalius grave hunting, and represents another big chunk out of my life.

As becomes obvious from the statues of Mercator and Vesalius in the hall of fame in the façade of the Leuven Renaissance town hall, men in tights carrying a world globe or a skull really look alike.

Their quest, be it to the inside or to the outside, looks very similar. Isn't that exactly what Vesalius also told his patron: '… (man as) the place and the instrument of the immortal soul: a home that is amazingly similar to the universe'?"

To bring to his biography of the 18th-century anatomist Henry Gray and his illustrator Henry Vandyke Carter an extra pound of flesh, the American author Bill Hayes followed courses in anatomy. Thanks to this *The Anatomist: a true story of Gray's Anatomy* has surpassed the mere biographical record of his subject and himself. In the process of writing, Hayes also met himself. Not only the dissecting of bodies confronted him with death, but the ultimate confrontation came when his life partner died towards the end of book. 'Looking back, I can see how my whole life has led to this (book).'

'Anatomy is destiny,' Hayes says, paraphrasing Freud.

In contrast to the story of Hayes our journey does not end in death. A grave, empty, lost or yet to be found, is a continuing inspiration for the artists and scientists who share their work with us, for which I'm eternally grateful: Vesalius Continuum, remember? I hope that my fellow travellers, in search of the grave, also met themselves, as in: 'Have you found Vesalius yet? No, but I found a little bit more of myself.'

Now, this tombtourist only speaks for himself: if anatomy is indeed destiny, this quest for the lost grave of the father of anatomy, against all odds, does not end in death, but in curiosity, understanding, beauty, love, passion, life.

– from Athens to Zakynthos, Spring 2014

Illus. 17: Musician Arion saved by a dolphin: Printer Oporinus's device in the Fabrica of Vesalius.

Three occasional poems celebrating Andreas Vesalius in 1902, 1964 and 2014

Vesalius in Zante

SET wide the window. Let me drink the day.
I loved light ever, light in eye and brain –
No tapers mirrored in long palace floors,
Nor dedicated depths of silent aisles,
But just the common dusty wind-blown day
That roofs earth's millions.
O, too long I walked
In that thrice-sifted air that princes breathe,
Nor felt the heaven-wide jostling of the winds
And all the ancient outlawry of earth!
Now let me breathe and see.
This pilgrimage
They call a penance – let them call it that!
I set my face to the East to shrive my soul
Of mortal sin? So be it. If my blade
Once questioned living flesh, if once I tore
The pages of the Book in opening it,
See what the torn page yielded ere the light
Had paled its buried characters – and judge!

The girl they brought me, pinioned hand and foot
In catalepsy – say I should have known
That trance had not yet darkened into death,
And held my scalpel. Well, suppose I *knew?*
Sum up the facts – her life against her death.
Her life? The scum upon the pools of pleasure
Breeds such by thousands. And her death? Perchance

The obolus to appease the ferrying Shade,
And waft her into immortality.
Think what she purchased with that one heart-flutter
That whispered its deep secret to my blade!
For, just because her bosom fluttered still,
It told me more than many rifled graves;

Because I spoke too soon, she answered me,
Her vain life ripened to this bud of death
As the whole plant is forced into one flower,
All her blank past a scroll on which God wrote
His word of healing – so that the poor flesh,
Which spread death living, died to purchase life!

Ah, no! The sin I sinned was mine, not theirs.
Not *that* they sent me forth to wash away –
None of their tariffed frailties, but a deed
So far beyond their grasp of good or ill
That, set to weigh it in the Church's balance,
Scarce would they know which scale to cast it in.
But I, I know. I sinned against my will,
Myself, my soul – the God within the breast:
Can any penance wash such sacrilege?

When I was young in Venice, years ago,
I walked the hospice with a Spanish monk,
A solitary cloistered in high thoughts,
The great Loyola, whom I reckoned then
A mere refurbisher of faded creeds,
Expert to edge anew the arms of faith,
As who should say, a Galenist, resolved
To hold the walls of dogma against fact,
Experience, insight, his own self, if need be!
Ah, how I pitied him, mine own eyes set
Straight in the level beams of Truth, who groped
In error's old deserted catacombs
And lit his tapers upon empty graves!
Ay, but he held his own, the monk – more man
Than any laurelled cripple of the wars,
Charles's spent shafts; for what he willed he willed,
As those do that forerun the wheels of fate,
Not take their dust – that force the virgin hours,
Hew life into the likeness of themselves
And wrest the stars from their concurrences.
So firm his mould; but mine the ductile soul
That wears the livery of circumstance

And hangs obsequious on its suzerain's eye.
For who rules now? The twilight-flitting monk,
Or I, that took the morning like an Alp?
He held his own, I let mine slip from me,
The birthright that no sovereign can restore;
And so ironic Time beholds us now
Master and slave – he lord of half the earth,
I ousted from my narrow heritage.

For there's the sting! My kingdom knows me not.
Reach me that folio – my usurper's title!
Fallopius reigning, *vice* – nay, not so:
Successor, not usurper. I am dead.
My throne stood empty; he was heir to it.
Ay, but who hewed his kingdom from the waste,
Cleared, inch by inch, the acres for his sowing,
Won back for man that ancient fief o' the Church,
His body? Who flung Galen from his seat,
And founded the great dynasty of truth
In error's central kingdom?
Ask men that,
And see their answer: just a wondering stare,
To learn things were not always as they are –
The very fight forgotten with the fighter;
Already grows the moss upon my grave!
Ay, and so meet – hold fast to that, Vesalius.
They only, who re-conquer day by day
The inch of ground they camped on over-night,
Have right of foothold on this crowded earth.
I left mine own; he seized it; with it went
My name, my fame, my very self, it seems,
Till I am but the symbol of a man,
The sign-board creaking o'er an empty inn.
He names me – true! *'Oh, give the door its due*
I entered by. Only, my masters, note,
Had door been none, a shoulder-thrust of mine
Had breached the crazy wall' – he seems to say.
So meet – and yet a word of thanks, of praise,
Of recognition that the clue was found,

Seized, followed, clung to, by some hand now dust –
Had this obscured his quartering of my shield?

How the one weakness stirs again! I thought
I had done with that old thirst for gratitude
That lured me to the desert years ago
I did my work – and was not that enough?
No; but because the idlers sneered and shrugged,
The envious whispered, the traducers lied,
And friendship doubted where it should have cheered,
I flung aside the unfinished task, sought praise
Outside my soul's esteem, and learned too late
That victory, like God's kingdom, is within.
(Nay, let the folio rest upon my knee.
I do not feel its weight.) Ingratitude?
The hurrying traveller does not ask the name
Of him who points him on his way; and this
Fallopius sits in the mid-heart of me,
Because he keeps his eye upon the goal,
Cuts a straight furrow to the end in view,
Cares not who oped the fountain by the way,
But drinks to draw fresh courage for his journey.
That was the lesson that Ignatius taught –
The one I might have learned from him, but would not –
That we are but stray atoms on the wind,
A dancing transiency of summer eves,
Till we become one with our purpose, merged
In that vast effort of the race which makes
Mortality immortal.
'He that loseth
His life shall find it': so the Scripture runs.
But I so hugged the fleeting self in me,
So loved the lovely perishable hours,
So kissed myself to death upon their lips,
That on one pyre we perished in the end –
A grimmer bonfire than the Church e'er lit!
Yet all was well – or seemed so – till I heard
That younger voice, an echo of my own,
And, like a wanderer turning to his home,

Who finds another on the hearth, and learns,
Half-dazed, that other is his actual self
In name and claim, as the whole parish swears,
So strangely, suddenly, stood dispossessed
Of that same self I had sold all to keep,
A baffled ghost that none would see or hear!
'Vesalius? Who's Vesalius? This Fallopius
It is who dragged the Galen-idol down,
Who rent the veil of flesh and forced a way
Into the secret fortalice of life' –
Yet it was I that bore the brunt of it!

Well, better so! Better awake and live
My last brief moment, as the man I was,
Than lapse from life's long lethargy to death
Without one conscious interval. At least
I repossess my past, am once again
No courtier med'cining the whims of kings
In muffled palace-chambers, but the free
Friendless Vesalius, with his back to the wall
And all the world against him. O, for that
Best gift of all, Fallopius, take my thanks –
That, and much more. At first, when Padua wrote:
'Master, Fallopius dead, resume again
The chair even he could not completely fill,
And see what usury age shall take of youth
In honors forfeited' – why, just at first,
I was quite simply credulously glad
To think the old life stood ajar for me,
Like a fond woman's unforgetting heart.
But now that death waylays me – now I know
This isle is the circumference of my days,
And I shall die here in a little while –
So also best, Fallopius!
For I see
The gods may give anew, but not restore;
And though I think that, in my chair again,
I might have argued my supplanters wrong
In this or that – this Cesalpinus, say,

With all his hot-foot blundering in the dark,
Fabricius, with his over-cautious clutch
On Galen (systole and diastole
Of Truth's mysterious heart!) – yet, other ways,
It may be that this dying serves the cause.
For Truth stays not to build her monument
For this or that co-operating hand,
But props it with her servants' failures – nay,
Cements its courses with their blood and brains,
A living substance that shall clinch her walls
Against the assaults of time. Already, see,
Her scaffold rises on my hidden toil,
I but the accepted premiss whence must spring
The airy structure of her argument;
Nor could the bricks it rests on serve to build
The crowning finials. I abide her law:
A different substance for a different end –
Content to know I hold the building up;
Though men, agape at dome and pinnacles,
Guess not, the whole must crumble like a dream
But for that buried labor underneath.
Yet, Padua, I had still my word to say!
Let others say it! – Ah, but will they guess
Just the one word – ? Nay, Truth is many-tongued.
What one man failed to speak, another finds
Another word for. May not all converge
In some vast utterance, of which you and I,
Fallopius, were but halting syllables?
So knowledge come, no matter how it comes!
No matter whence the light falls, so it fall!
Truth's way, not mine – that I, whose service failed
In action, yet may make amends in praise.
Fabricius, Cesalpinus, say your word,
Not yours, or mine, but Truth's, as you receive it!
You miss a point I saw? See others, then!
Misread my meaning? Yet expound your own!
Obscure one space I cleared? The sky is wide,
And you may yet uncover other stars.

For thus I read the meaning of this end:
There are two ways of spreading light; to be
The candle or the mirror that reflects it.
I let my wick burn out – there yet remains
To spread an answering surface to the flame
That others kindle.

Turn me in my bed.
The window darkens as the hours swing round;
But yonder, look, the other casement glows!
Let me face westward as my sun goes down.

'Vesalius in Zante (1564)'
by Edith Wharton
North American Review 175 (Nov. 1902): 625–631.

To the great Belgian anatomist
Andreas Vesalius

In the sky of science shines illuminated
your memory, Andreas Vesalius, eternally.
They always honor and glorify You
through the years that come and pass by.

Why, you loved man and strove
to lessen rough pain.
With heart's faith, with self-denial
and with the light – Andreas Vesalius – of thought.

Deep darkness surrounded man.
Ignorance and prejudice, suffering, hatred
Apprehended light, persecuted him
so not to enlighten life's path.

But You, alike to all great figures, rose
and set the stepping ground.
For others to come on your trail
to build the temple of science.

You were both precursor and martyr.
This is always so in life's story.
The bridges of good to consolidate
seek for the most precious sacrifice.

You, Grand benefactor of humanity
and honoured child of Belgium
who were thrown from the tide of life
to the angry wave of the sea.

To the Greek seacoast fate forsook you
in the blue colour of our sky.
And as an affectionate mother sweetly covered you
the fragrant soil of Zakynthos.

'To the great Belgian anatomist Andreas Vesalius'
by Crysanthi Zitsaia.
Occasional poem written for the Vesalius commoration in Zakynthos in May 1965,
(from the private collection of Dr. Emmanuel Corcondilas; publication unknown),
translated from Greek into English in 2014 by Lefkothea-Vasiliki Andreou.

Vesalius

if Galen was alive to-day
he'd turn in his grave
all his ideas smashed to pieces
by the Flemish upstart
but no
think again professor
he'd be man enough and more to celebrate with joy
the 500th birthday
how time passes
of his supplanter his usurper
his successor
ever the philosopher he

for it seemed fair to assume that monkey
ape and pig and dog are not different inside to humans
in many cases our behaviour is very similar indeed
and why would the gods have gone to so much trouble
to change things between these creatures and our deer selves
and how was Galen to know
(maybe mice are not the same as men and time will laugh itself silly
at our modern experiments and well made plans)

a lot of blood was let under the bridge to flow and not in vein
quite another stream of thought in fact
to lower the humour of the sanguine tensions
but nobody was laughing
he was a man after the truth
but the truth came after him
a cut above the others
not he the bigot and the closed minded one
'twas follower admirer and disciple who had that distinction
it took a great man to shake them out of their chairs
and to kick them out of the university doors
a very special man indeed
brave or angry or both
who would open the human body of research to reveal

and to thrust their faces right into
the reality of our being

Vesalius
a man of those fleeting times
who rammed the past like a one man boarding crew
and the great learne'd master of antiquity was left at sea
and right behind poured all the 16th century die-hards
who went down with his ship
years before Vesalius went down with his
which by the by he didn't apparently
he survived the passage so they think
and died probably of scurvy on this lovely island in Greece
where now they meet in humility and praise to celebrate and to pay homage

1514–1564
hardly time enough to take on the world
hardly time enough to alter the mind and body of mankind
but he did it
a man of muscle and sinew and nerve and guts
bone idle never and with no skeletons in his cupboard
and all the vital organs of state behind him or on his side or fronting for him
he spent his life delving into the amazing body of research that he left behind
for the quick to get clear in their head cells
a corporal discoverer who suffered fools not a corpuscle
went for the jugular and knew exactly where it was and by the way still is
soon word circulated
the heart and soul of an anatomist
with the force of a surgeon screaming for a swab to a dreaming lovelorn nurse
and the arrogance of an over-active thighrod
he pulsed through the world
until medics of every country were shouting
Vesalius Vesalius
he got so they say a little too close to the life of luxury
in the last middle leg of his career
and needed an upholstered rest
not easy to operate on the established past
with no anaesthetic and against its will
and the enemy afoot

with only a blunt idea with which to open old wounds
and to slice through the pampered skin of the unquestioning

and now
hundreds of years later they look to this man
his beautiful books of anatomy still ring the bell
and never before or since was there such a man
we think of him as genius
the brave and bold adventurer
the creator of the modern approach to medicine
they search for his bones to recreate his image
they honour his memory to express their admiration
they treasure his books to learn the better to emulate him
they bow down to his great achievements
Vesalius
master of anatomy
hero of mankind
genius of the inner self
who got under the skin of mankind at a very early age and
brought us to our senses
and everything

but Galen was no fool
and many of his operations are still closely close
to those performed in modern times
especially the eyes
he got the circulation a bit wrong so we're told
but it was a very long time ago
and things have changed a lot since then

from Galen to Vesalius to…whom
is there somebody out there who is about to reveal something extraordinary
about our bodies
the brain doesn't exist
for example or
the heart so called is in fact nothing but a pulsating lump of fat
that we inherited for no good reason from fish
our stomachs are in our heads that's why we burp
and we think with our private parts

anything is possible
certainly a lot of people think with their private parts
but it's more abstract these days
like maybe we are living out a thousand possible lives
in this hologram of a black hole
and Dr. Quantum tells us that things behave differently when observed
so let's stop looking too closely at each other looking backwards
and jump (with a rope around the waist)
into the artesiance
of Art and Science

which while we're at it
should be a pain between the ears
to amalgamate art and science
what a business
nobody can say what art is
(we know what it was)
and nobody knows where science is going
(we know where it's been)
and people talk glibly about doing art and science
what on earth could that be
it is a pain between the ears
an incredible challenge
worthy of a lifetime of struggle
we need to create hospitals by the well
to nurse the brave souls who take on this daunting plunge
for there will be casualties
or there should be
if it is done properly
(some might kick the bucket even)
for it is very deep
and dark
and maybe
after years and years
somebody will dip into the cure for everything
imagine how silly we will feel
if it turns out that ill health is totally avoidable
for thousands of years mankind has suffered
and all we needed all along

CONCLUSION: TO BE CONTINUED...

was a sip of flea's sperm mixed with humble pie
a little each day
to live healthily forever
let's drink to the great men of biology and medicine and anatomy
they saved our skin and will do so hopefully until the cows come home
no wish to milk it but anybody over the age of thirty-five
and anybody under the age of thirty-five
and anybody of exactly the age of thirty-five
probably owes their existence to
man's study of his fellow man
and in particular
Andreas Vesalius
who
by luck or judgement we may never know
chose to study the very fellow human, the very geezer, whose interior set-up
was just right for the books

if Vesalius was alive today
he'd be scrutinizing his corpse in its grave
extracting DNA (Do Not Alter)
and reconstructing the future as the sigh 'clone' passes overhead and
heals everybody's dolly in a brain storm
for between two well established extremes
lies nonsense in all its glory
and the wonderful act of splashing
(this theory floats upon a misunderstanding of the theme of a lecture from a famous
Oxford scholar who, as it turned out, is fascinated by the beautiful architectural
structures created by this activity)
splashing – put a hand into each pool of thought
(we used to talk of fields of research but that was far too dry
for the tide of new across-the-fence ideas of a fluid nature)
for the grass on the other side is always bogged down in a wetter greenery
put a hand in each pool of thought
now toss the contents high into the limelight
and watch what happens as they mingle
flood and mingle again
and land for the most part outside of the vessel from which they sprang
thus think of art and science as liquid
and you're half way home

like a liquid lunch solves most of life's problems
whilst causing others
and the pain between the ears avoided
by a child-like fascination for what happens next in your brain
thawed out thoughts
swirling around the pillars of wisdom
flooding the universities' base-meant flaw and
washing away the foundations of
elephantine ivory towers
dripping into sulphuric history to the brim even
rotting the cover ups and downs and going to press the turn-up for the books
and the trousers of the pulled leg and the stone in the sock and the one boned jaw

not
'preparing the ground for the future'
as we used to put it
but
topping up the puddles of our being and
waving towards our nothingness
our everythingness
our oceanic drop
our watery two-dimensional
grid

Vesalius
1514-1564

by Bryan W. Green, 2013,
http://www.vesaliusfabrica.com/en/vesalius/truth-and-myth/vesalius-poem.html

Endnotes

1   BIESBROUCK, Maurits, Theodoor GODDEERIS, Omer STEENO. 'The Last Months of Andreas Vesalius: a Coda' in Vesalius - Acta Internationalia Historiae Medicinae, 2012, 18 (no. 2): 70-75, ill.

2   BIESBROUCK, Maurits, Omer STEENO, 'The Last Months of Andreas Vesalius' in Vesalius Acta Internationalia Historiae Medicinae, 2010, Dec; 16 (2): 100-6

3   http://www.vesaliusfabrica.com/en/vesalius/history-context/vesalius-religion.html

4   Itinerarium Aegypti, Arabiae, Palaestinae, Syriae, aliarumque regionum orientalium, [Traveling in Egypt, Arabia, Palestine, Syria, and other Eastern countries]   Nuremberg 1621, pp.2. See: http://books.google.co.uk/books/about/Itinerarium_Aegypti_Arabiae_Palestinae_S.html?id=SnMPpOjb5DgC&redir_esc=y.

5   Il devotissimo Viaggio Di Gierusalemme, Rome 1595, pp. 85–86. See: http://books.google.co.uk/books/about/Il_devotissimo_Viaggio_Di_Gierusalemme.html?id=Z45AAAAQAAJ&redir_esc=y.

6   A copy of one of his letters, dated 12 July 1586 in Zante, is kept in the Biblioteca Ambrosiana of Milan.

7   Teatro del Mondo di A. Ortelio: da lui poco inanzi la sua morte riveduto, e di tavole nuove et commenti adorno, et arricchito, con la vita dell' autore. Traslato in lingua Toscana dal Sigr F. Pigafetta, 1608/1612, map 217.
    A photograph of the Italian text was very kindly sent to me by Dr Marcel van den Broecke. The original is kept in the Dutch Royal Library (Koninklijke Bibliotheek), in The Hague, the Netherlands.

8   Because Pigafetta's reference appears to be unknown to Vesalius researchers I quote the whole passage in my own translation.

9   The photographs are not not included in this book; they are, however, published on Plessas's blogspot: http://pampalaia.blogspot.gr/search/label/Andreas%20Vesalius?updated-max=2012-12-27T01:51:00%2B02:00&max-results=20&start=5&by-date=false

10 Παρνασσός; Vol 14, No 10 (1892) pp. 634. See: http://openarchives.gr/view/204733

11 Sole author of this chapter 25 is Sylviane Déderix, Research Fellow of the National Fund for Scientific Research (F.R.S.-FNRS), Université Catholique de Louvain/INCAL/CEMA/AEGIS Research Group, Laboratory of Geophysical - Satellite Remote Sensing & Archaeo-environment (IMS-FORTH. Her PhD, with success defended in April 2014, consists of a GIS-based study of the funerary landscapes of Bronze Age in Crete.

12 These re-examinations, by Omer Steeno, Maurits Biesbrouck, Theodoor Goddeeris and Pavlos Plessas, focused on sources dated shortly after Vesalius's death. In addition to the well-known reference in Petrus Bizarus's book Pannonicum Bellum, 1573, pp. 284–285, and Johannes Metellus's letter to Georgius Cassander in 1565 from Petrus Bertius's Illustrium & clarorum Virorum Epistolae Selectiores, 1617, pp. 372–373, the letter of Metellus to Arnoldus Birckmannus, dated 1565, from a manuscript kept in the John Crerar Library; and a 1566 letter of Reinerus Solenander found in Thomas Theodor Crusius's Vergnügung müssiger Stunden, oder allerhand nutzliche zur heutigen galanten Gelehrsamkeit dienende Anmerckungen, 1722, and translated into English in 'The Last Months of Andreas Vesalius: a Coda' by Biesbrouck, Goddeeris and Steeno (Vesalius – Acta Internationalia Historiae Medicinae, volume XVIII, December 2012, pp. 70–75) were also re-examined.

13 Two sources name this church as the burial place of Vesalius: Christoph Fürer von Haimendorf's Itinerarium Aegypti, Arabiae, Palaestinae, Syriae, aliarumque Regionum Orientalium, 1621, pp. 2, detailing the author's journey of 1565, and Giovanni Zuallardo's Il devotissimo Viaggio Di

Gierusalemme, 1595, pp. 85-86, from a visit of the author to Zakynthos in 1586. Two more sources indirectly place Vesalius's grave in Santa Maria delle Grazie: the letter of Solenander mentioned in the previous note and a comment by Filippo Pigafetta in the *Teatro del Mondo di A. Ortelio: da lui poco inanzi la sua morte riveduto, e di tavole nuove et commenti adorno, et arricchito, con la vita dell' autore*. Traslato in lingua Toscana dal Sigr F. Pigafetta, 1608/1612. The comment was entered as background information of Map 217 and there is no indication of when Pigafetta saw the grave. It is assumed, however, that it was many years earlier; Pigafetta was already dead when this work was published.

14   Nikolaos Katramis, Φιλολογικά Ανάλεκτα Ζακύνθου, 1880, pp. 455.

15   Leonidas Zoes, Λεξικόν Ιστορικόν και Λαογραφικόν Ζακύνθου, volume 1, 1963, pp. 509.

16   Giovanni Zuallardo, *Il devotissimo Viaggio Di Gierusalemme*, 1595, pp. 85–86.

17   http://pampalaia.blogspot.co.uk/2012/08/blog-post.html

18   Plan of the 'Citta del Zanthe', drawn 15 December 1632, by Nicolò Gentilini, on a scale of 60 paces to an inch, British Library; plan of the monastery from 1806 from Επτάνησος Πολιτεία (1800–1807), έκδοση της Νομαρχιακής Αυτοδιοίκησης Κέρκυρας, ΓΑΚ – Αρχεία Νομού Κέρκυρας, Κέρκυρα 2000; Dionysios Zivas, Η αρχιτεκτονική της Ζακύνθου από τον ΙΣΤ' μέχρι τον ΙΘ' αιώνα, 1970, pic. 41; pre-earthquake diagram of Zakynthos updated with the latest cadastral information, May 1954, Διεύθυνσις Τοπογραφήσεων και Κτηματολογίου.

19   Conolly J., 2008. 'Geographical Information Systems and Landscape Archaeology' in David B. & Thomas J. (eds.), *Handbook of Landscape Archaeology* (World Archaeological Congress. Research Handbooks in Archaeology 1), Walnut Creek, pp. 583.

20   See for instance Jones C., 1997. *Geographical Information Systems and Computer Cartography*, Harlow, pp. 3–17; Longley P.A., Goodchild M.F., Maguire D.J. & Rhind D.W., 2005. *Geographic Information Systems and Science*, Chichester, pp. 35–60.

21   For a brief history of archaeological uses of GIS, see for instance Harris T.M. & Lock G.R., 1995. Towards an Evaluation of GIS in European Archaeology: The Past, Present and Future of Theory and Applications. *In*: Lock G. & Stančič Z. (eds), *Archaeology and GIS: A European Perspective*, London, p. 349-365; Wheatley D. & Gillings M., 2002. *Spatial Technology and Archaeology. The Archaeological Applications of GIS*, London, New York: pp. 16-20; Chapman H., 2006. *Landscape Archaeology and GIS*, Stroud: pp. 17-25; Conolly J. 2008 'Geographical Information Systems and Landscape Archaeology' in David B. & Thomas J. (eds.), *Handbook of Landscape Archaeology* (World Archaeological Congress. Research Handbooks in Archaeology 1), Walnut Creek, pp. 583–595.

22   For recent examples, see Fairen-Jimenez S., 2007. 'British Neolithic Rock Art in its Landscape', *Journal of Field Archaeology* 32, pp. 283–295; Llobera M. et al., 2010. 'Calculating the Inherent Visual Structure of a Landscape ('Total Viewshed') using High-throughput Computing' in Niccolucci F. & and Hermon S. (eds.), *Beyond the Artefact: Digital Interpretation of the Past. Proceedings of the 32nd CAA Conference, held in Prato (Italy), 13-17 April 2004*, Budapest, pp. 146–151; Wheatley D.W. et al., 2010. 'Approaching the Landscape Dimension of the Megalithic Phenomenon in Southern Spain', *OJA* 29, pp. 387–405; Bevan A., 2011. 'Computational Models for Understanding Movement and Territory' in Mayoral Herrera V. & Celestino Pérez S. (eds.), *Tecnologias de informacion geografica y analisis arqueologico del territorio: Actas del V Simposio Internacional de Arqueologia de Merida*, Merida, pp. 383–394; Winter-Livneh R. et al., 2012. 'Secondary Burial Cemeteries, Visibility and Land Tenure: A View from the Southern Levant Chalcolithic Period', *Journal of Anthropological Archaeology* 31, pp. 423–438.

23   Wheatley D. & Gillings M., 2002. Spatial Technology and Archaeology. The Archaeological Applications of GIS, London, New York: 25–28.

24   Zivas D., 2002. Η αρχιτεκτονική της Ζακύνθου από τον ΙΣΤ' μέχρι τον ΙΘ' αιώνα, 3rd edition, Athens, pl. 41.

List of illustrations and credits

Cover: 'Zante' from Carlo Maggi, *Voyages et aventures*, 1578. Bibliothèque nationale de France, département Estampes et photographie, RESERVE 4-AD-134

Black and white illustrations:

Illus. 1:   Title page, plate 5 from Andreas Vesalius, *De humani corporis fabrica libri septem*, Joannes Oporinus: Basel, 1543. Hendrik Conscience Heritage Library, Antwerp, cat. nr. J 5833.

Illus. 2:   Pattern of (the gradient of) fibers in a vein wall, details of plate 190, idem.

Illus. 3:   Male torso, plate 248, idem.

Illus. 4:   Skeleton contemplating, plate 93, idem.

Illus. 5:   Skeleton digging, plate 92, idem.

Illus. 6:   Portrait of Vesalius, plate 11, idem.

Illus. 7:   Old photograph of the lost Barbianis Monument in Kalogerata.

Illus. 8:   Old photograph, 'on the beach of Laganas', May 1, 1965, private collection Spiros Gaoutsis, Corfu, Greece.

Illus. 9:   Old photograph, 'on the Andre Vesal Square', May 2, 1965, idem.

Illus. 10:   Stealing cadavers in the initial letter L, plate 38, idem.

Illus. 11:   A turning point; the hinge, plate 44, idem.

Illus. 12:   From the monumental Fabrica, with scull, plate 29, idem.

Illus. 13:   Flay Man from Joannes Valverda, *De vivae imagines partium corporis humani, Plantijn*, Antwerp, 1566. Museum Plantin-Moretus, Antwerp, Unesco World Heritage Site.

Illus. 14:   Muscle Man, plate 98, idem.

Illus. 15:   Santa Maria delle Gracie before the earthquake, photograph private collection Spiros Gaoutsis, Corfu, Greece.

Illus. 16:   Figure 3, Geographical Information System, by Sylviane Déderix, for Laboratory of Geophysical-Satellite Remote Sensing & Archaeo-environment (IMS-FORTH), Crete, Greece.

Illus. 17:   Musician Arion saved by a dolphin; printer Oporinus's device in the Fabrica, plate 362, idem.

Section coloured photographs:

Illus. 1:   Facial reconstruction of Vesalius by Richard Neave and Pascale Pollier, photo courtesy St. George's University/Joshua Yetman, Grenada.

Illus. 2:   Franciscan stone, photo courtesy Maria Sidirokastriti, Zakynthos.

Illus. 3:   Coat of arms of Vesalius, sculpted by Chantal Pollier in Belgian marble.

Illus. 4:   Plinth of the new Vesalius monument in Zakynthos, sculpted by Chantal Pollier in Zakynthian stone.

Illus. 5:   Old well in Kalogerata, Laganas, photo courtesy Chantal Pollier

Illus. 6:   Figure 1, Geographical Information System, by Sylviane Déderix, for Laboratory of Geophysical-Satellite Remote Sensing & Archaeo-environment (IMS-FORTH), Crete, Greece.

Illus. 7:   Figure 2, GIS, idem.

Illus. 8:   Detail of the new Vesalius monument in Zakynthos, created by Richard Neave and Pascale Pollier; photo courtesy Jimmy Declercq, Kunstgieterij/ Fonderie De Clercq Ginsberg, Ghent, Belgium.